FACTOPEDIA TECHNOLOGY TRIVIA

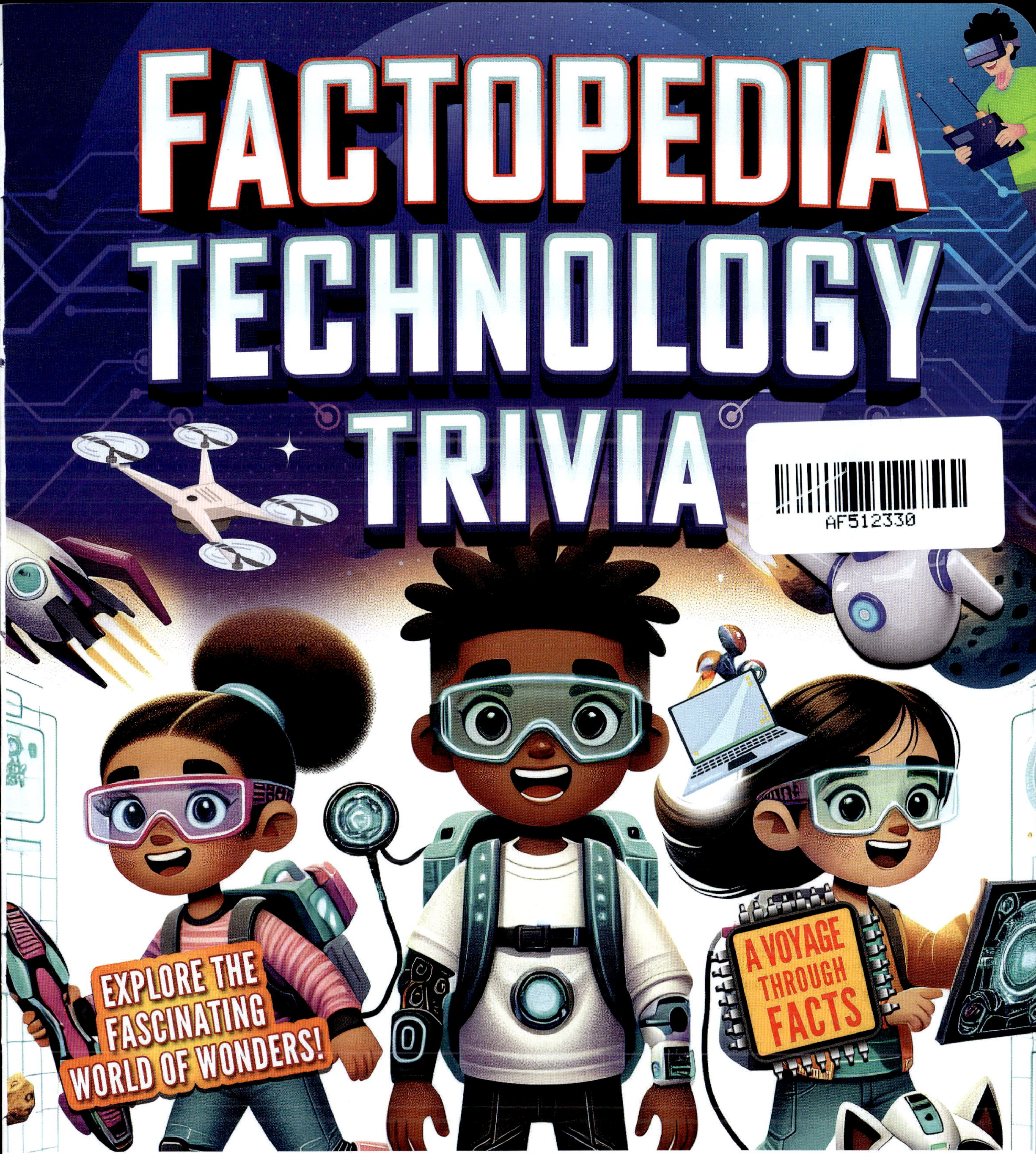

DREAMLAND PUBLICATIONS
J-128, Kirti Nagar, New Delhi - 110 015, India
Tel.: +91-11-2510 6050, 2543 5657
E-mail : dreamland@dreamlandpublications.com
Shop online at www.dreamlandpublications.com
Follow us on www.instagram.com/dreamland.publications

Published in 2025 by
DREAMLAND PUBLICATIONS
J-128, Kirti Nagar, New Delhi - 110 015, India
Tel : +91-11-2510 6050, 2543 5657
E-mail : dreamland@dreamlandpublications.com
www.dreamlandpublications.com

Printed in India

PREFACE

Welcome to **Factopedia—A Voyage Through Facts**, a captivating journey into the wonders of our world and beyond! This series is designed to spark curiosity and expand knowledge through fascinating facts about animals, dinosaurs, space, technology, and science.

Each book in this series is packed with incredible discoveries, surprising truths, and mind-blowing information that will leave readers amazed. From the mysteries of nature to the marvels of human innovation, this collection explores a wide range of topics in an engaging and easy-to-understand way.

Whether you love exploring the animal kingdom, uncovering the secrets of the universe, or diving into groundbreaking inventions, **Factopedia** has something for everyone. Get ready to embark on an exciting adventure through facts and let your curiosity lead the way!

CONTENTS

What does technology mean, and why do we need it?

Technology means using tools, machines, and inventions created by people to make life easier and better. We need technology to solve problems, save time, connect with others, and help us learn, build, travel, and stay healthy. It improves the way we live every day!

ANCIENT TOOLS VS. MODERN TECHNOLOGY

In ancient times, people invented tools like the wheel to make transportation easier. Today, we use advanced technology like cars and airplanes to travel long distances quickly and comfortably.

TECH IN DAILY LIFE

Microwaves cook meals fast, and video calls keep us connected with loved ones anywhere.

DIFFERENT KINDS OF TECHNOLOGY

Transportation technology includes vehicles like cars and airplanes. Communication technology covers things like phones and emails. Medical technology involves equipment like X-rays and life-saving vaccines.

BRAIN BUZZ

- What do you need for a video call?
- Can smartwatches help in daily life?
- What powers most home gadgets?

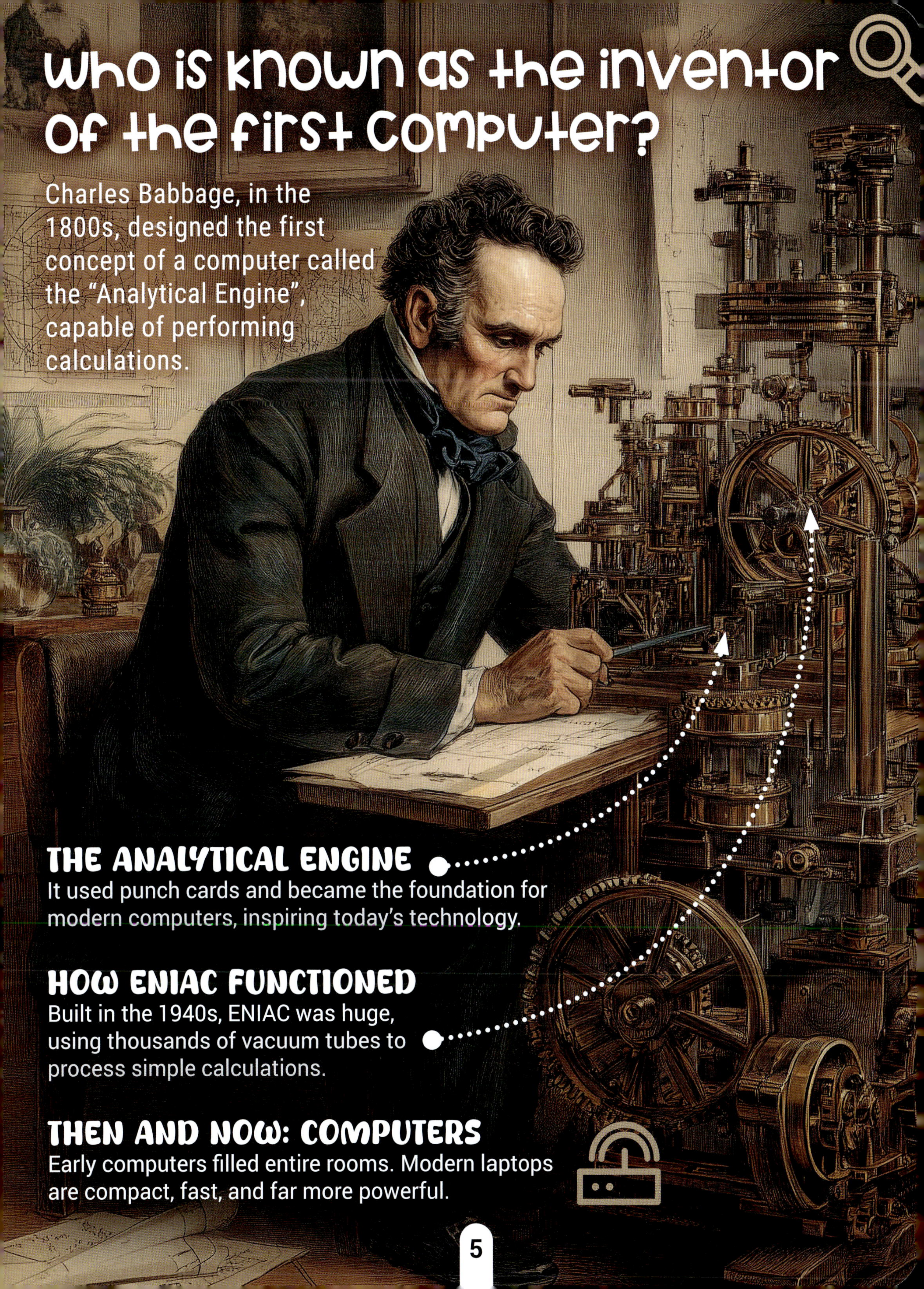

Who is known as the inventor of the first computer?

Charles Babbage, in the 1800s, designed the first concept of a computer called the "Analytical Engine", capable of performing calculations.

THE ANALYTICAL ENGINE

It used punch cards and became the foundation for modern computers, inspiring today's technology.

HOW ENIAC FUNCTIONED

Built in the 1940s, ENIAC was huge, using thousands of vacuum tubes to process simple calculations.

THEN AND NOW: COMPUTERS

Early computers filled entire rooms. Modern laptops are compact, fast, and far more powerful.

What technology powers smartphones?

Smartphones are compact yet advanced devices that let you make calls, send messages, surf the internet, and use various apps. They rely on powerful microprocessors and smart sensors to perform all these tasks seamlessly.

RESPONSIVE TOUCHSCREENS

Touch-sensitive screens detect your fingers and turn taps or swipes into instant actions.

POWERFUL PROCESSORS

The processor, often called the brain of the phone, performs millions of tasks quickly to run apps, calls, and videos.

FUN FACT

IBM SIMON, THE FIRST SMARTPHONE, INTRODUCED IN 1992, HAD BASIC APPS AND A TOUCHSCREEN!

BRAIN BUZZ

- What is a smartphone processor?
- What powers a smartphone?
- What makes touchscreens work?

How does Wi-Fi connect devices to the internet?

Wi-Fi uses invisible radio waves to wirelessly transfer data between your devices and the internet, without needing cables.

SIGNAL STRENGTH & DISTANCE

Wi-Fi speed depends on how close you are to the router. Walls and distance can weaken the connection.

BRAIN BUZZ

- Can Wi-Fi signals pass through walls?
- What is needed to set up Wi-Fi?
- Is Wi-Fi faster closer to the router?

FUN FACT

THE TERM WI-FI DOESN'T MEAN ANYTHING! IT WAS CREATED TO SOUND LIKE "HI-FI," WHICH REFERS TO HIGH-FIDELITY SOUND.

THE ROLE OF A ROUTER

A router links your devices to the internet. Think of it as a hub that directs where data should go.

HOW RADIO WAVES WORK

Wi-Fi uses radio signals to send and receive information, similar to how walkie-talkies communicate.

How does Cloud Computing Work?

Cloud computing works by storing and managing data on remote servers accessed via the internet. This lets people save files, run programs, and collaborate without needing powerful personal devices.

HOW CLOUD WORKS

Information is saved on distant servers, which you can reach online. This saves space on your personal devices.

EVERYDAY USES

The cloud supports email, file sharing, video streaming, online gaming, and more.

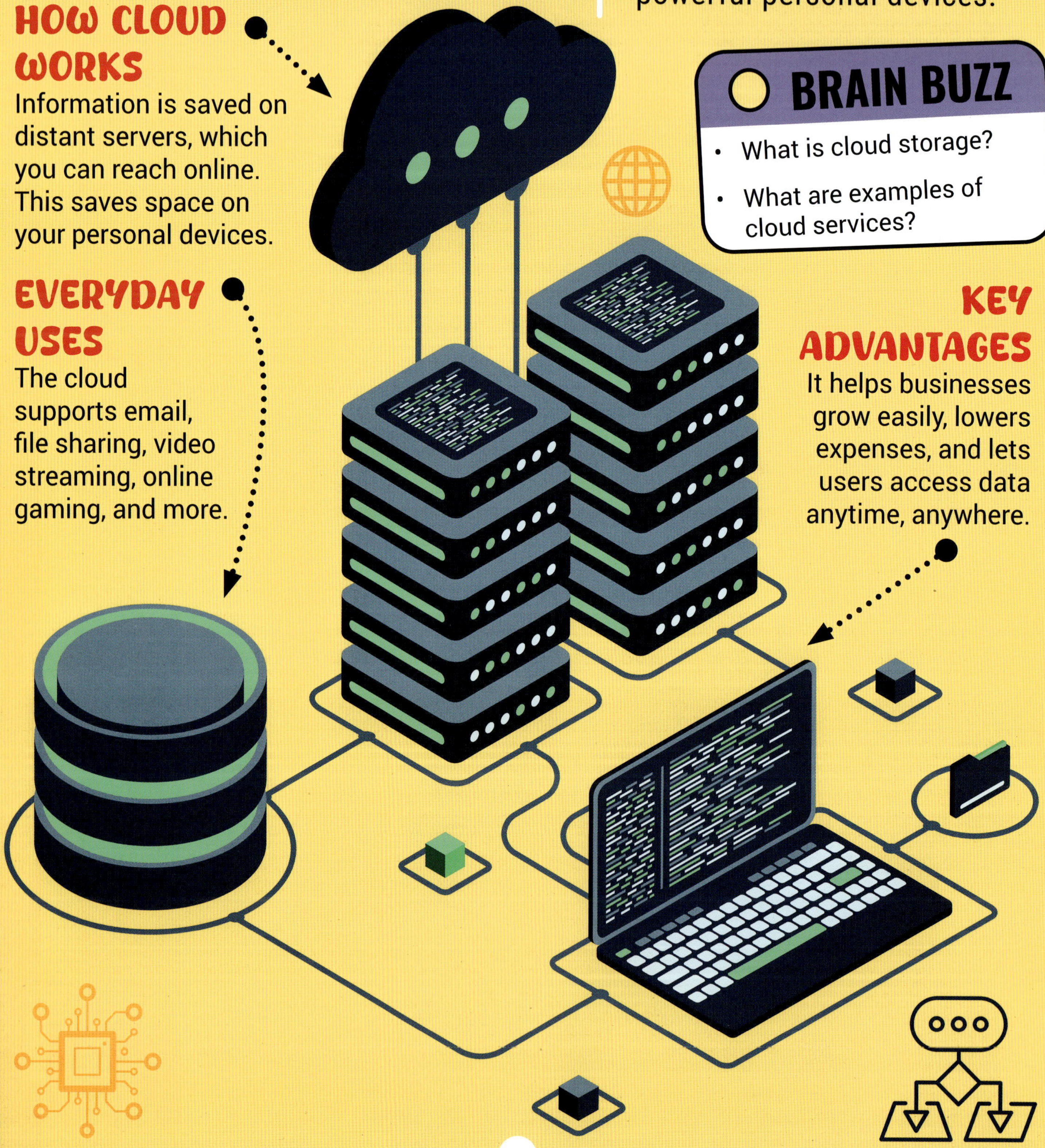

BRAIN BUZZ

- What is cloud storage?
- What are examples of cloud services?

KEY ADVANTAGES

It helps businesses grow easily, lowers expenses, and lets users access data anytime, anywhere.

What is the fifth generation (5G) network?

The fifth generation (5G) network is a faster, more reliable wireless technology. It connects devices quickly and improves internet speed for smoother communication.

HOW 5G OPERATES

5G transmits data using high-frequency radio waves, allowing much faster speeds than 4G.

REAL-WORLD USES

It powers smart cities, self-driving cars, and enables seamless streaming of ultra HD videos.

KEY ADVANTAGES

5G offers lightning-fast downloads, minimal delays, and supports many devices at the same time.

BRAIN BUZZ

- How fast is 5G?
- Can 5G support more devices?
- Where is 5G used?

What does IoT mean?

IoT stands for the Internet of Things. It describes a network of devices—like smart appliances, wearables, and sensors—that connect to the internet and share data. These devices work together to make life more convenient, efficient, and smart.

BRAIN BUZZ

- How do IoT devices communicate?
- Is IoT safe to use?
- Where is IoT used?

COMMON IOT DEVICES

Smart speakers, smart lights, fitness trackers, and thermostats connect to the internet to make life easier.

HOW IT OPERATES

IoT devices use sensors to gather data and communicate over Wi-Fi or other networks to complete tasks automatically.

EVERYDAY BENEFITS

IoT helps automate actions like switching off lights, locking doors, or watering plants, even when you're not home.

How does the Global Positioning System (GPS) find locations?

GPS works by receiving signals from multiple satellites in space. These signals help calculate your exact position on Earth and guide you to where you need to go.

ORBITING SATELLITES

More than 30 GPS satellites circle the Earth, sending signals that cover the whole planet.

HOW TRIANGULATION WORKS

Devices figure out your location by using signals from at least three satellites to pinpoint where you are.

FUN FACT

GPS IS SO PRECISE THAT SCIENTISTS TRACK TECTONIC PLATES AND STUDY NATURAL DISASTERS WITH IT.

COMMON GPS USES

GPS helps with car navigation, phone directions, and guides hikers in remote places.

What is Artificial Intelligence and how does it work?

Artificial Intelligence, or AI, is smart technology that allows machines to think, learn, and make decisions, similar to how people do.

AI IN DAILY LIFE

Artificial Intelligence helps us every day—voice assistants (like Alexa), smart searches (like Google), and movie suggestions (like Netflix).

HOW AI GETS SMARTER

AI learns by studying large amounts of data, just like people practice to get better at something.

WHAT'S NEXT FOR AI

In the future, AI may help cure diseases, explore space, and solve major global challenges.

FUN FACT

SOME AI PROGRAMS CAN COMPOSE MUSIC, WRITE POEMS, AND EVEN HELP DOCTORS DETECT DISEASES EARLY!

What are virtual assistants powered by AI?

Virtual assistants like Siri, Alexa, and Google Assistant use AI to follow voice commands. They help with tasks like setting alarms, playing music, or giving weather updates, making daily life easier.

HOW THEY FUNCTION

AI assistants listen to your voice, understand the words, and perform tasks or give answers.

COMMON USES

They help set alarms, play music, control smart home gadgets, and answer questions.

FUTURE POSSIBILITIES

AI helpers may soon detect feelings and give advice tailored just for you.

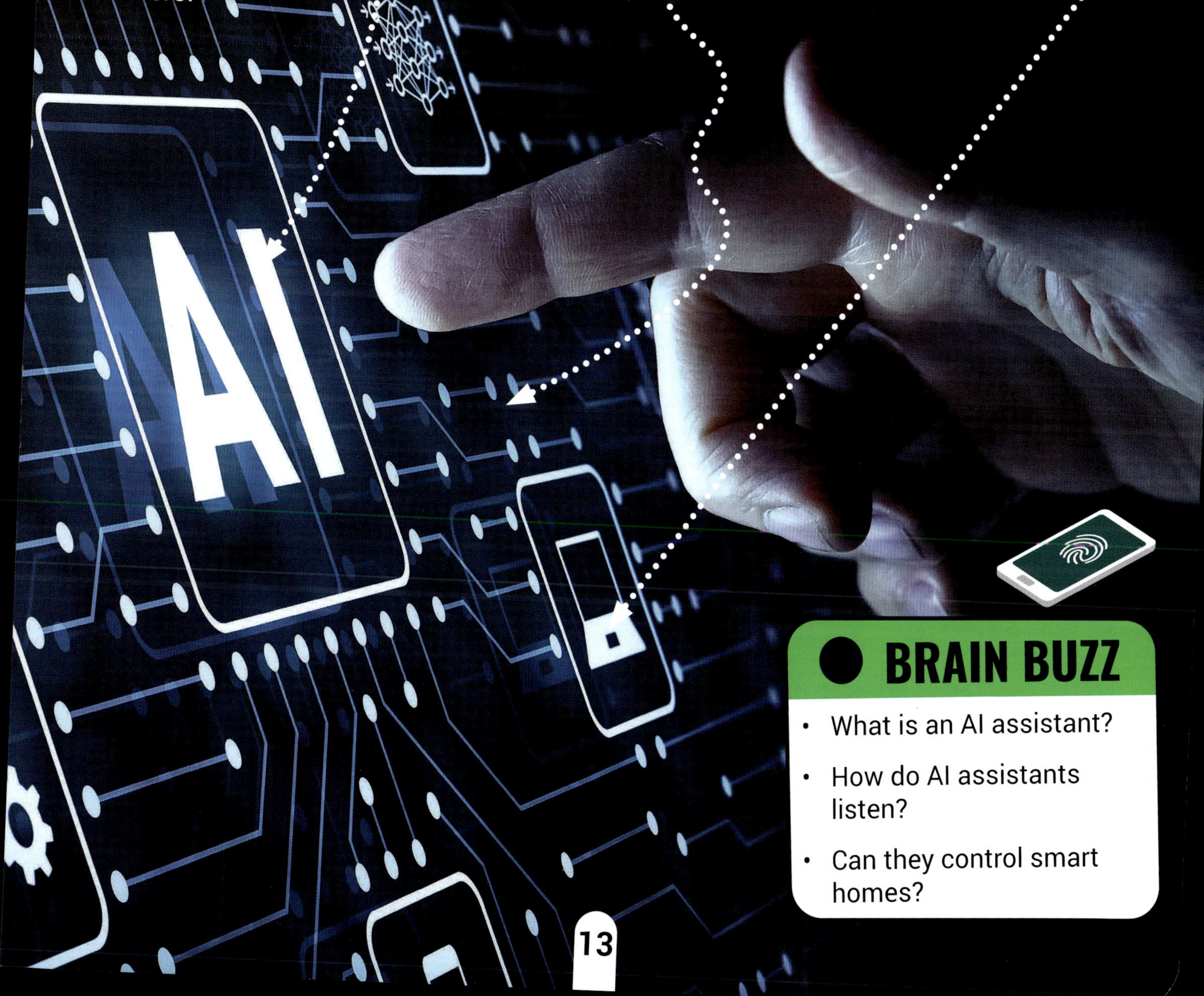

BRAIN BUZZ

- What is an AI assistant?
- How do AI assistants listen?
- Can they control smart homes?

What does Google Assistant do on a smartphone?

Google Assistant is a voice-controlled AI. It helps you call, text, set reminders, and search the web using just your voice.

UNDERSTANDING COMMANDS

They use AI and language processing to interpret your voice and respond with helpful actions.

EVERYDAY TASKS

You can ask them to send texts, set alarms, play songs, or give weather updates.

SMART HOME CONTROL

They connect with smart devices, letting you control lights, thermostats, and more by voice.

FUN FACT

APPLE'S SIRI, LAUNCHED IN 2011, WAS THE FIRST VOICE ASSISTANT TO BE BUILT INTO A SMARTPHONE!

How is AI used in video games?

AI in video games makes opponents smarter and gameplay more challenging. It learns player strategies and adapts, making games feel more real and exciting.

BEHIND THE SCENES

AI studies how players act and adjusts the game to keep it fun and challenging.

IN-GAME EXAMPLES

NPCs (Non-Player Characters) in games like chess or adventure games use AI to react and make smart choices.

WHAT'S NEXT?

Future games may have AI characters with unique personalities, making worlds feel more alive and interactive.

BRAIN BUZZ

- What are NPCs in games?
- How does AI make games harder?
- Can AI create games?

How does quantum computing work?

Quantum computing uses the principles of quantum mechanics to process information much faster than regular computers.

WHAT ARE QUBITS?

Qubits can hold many states at once, making quantum computers extremely powerful.

SUPER-FAST PROCESSING

Quantum computers solve complex problems in minutes that might take traditional computers years.

REAL-WORLD USES

They help design new medicines, streamline supply chains, and boost artificial intelligence.

FUN FACT

QUANTUM COMPUTERS MUST STAY SUPER COLD—NEAR ABSOLUTE ZERO—TO WORK CORRECTLY!

How does the quantum internet work?

The quantum internet uses quantum principles to transmit data quickly and securely, offering safer communication.

HOW IT FUNCTIONS

It uses quantum particles, such as photons, to send data securely—any tampering is instantly noticeable.

BRAIN BUZZ

- What makes quantum internet secure?
- Which particles carry data in quantum networks?
- Can quantum internet prevent hacking?

KEY BENEFITS

Delivers ultra-secure connections and promises faster, safer data sharing than regular internet.

WHAT'S AHEAD

May link powerful quantum computers worldwide, advancing science and technology.

How does blockchain technology work?

Blockchain is a secure digital ledger. It stores data in linked blocks, making transactions transparent and hard to change.

OTHER USES OF BLOCKCHAIN

Blockchain helps in secure voting, tracking goods in supply chains, and safeguarding health records.

NO CENTRAL CONTROL

Blockchains work on decentralized systems, meaning no single person or group runs it, boosting security.

BRAIN BUZZ

- Who validates blockchain transactions?
- What industries use blockchain?
- Can blockchain prevent fraud?

PROCESS EXPLAINED

Data is stored in blocks, linked together, and checked by many computers to ensure accuracy.

How does cryptocurrency work?

Cryptocurrency is digital money. It uses blockchain for secure, decentralized payments.

HOW IT OPERATES

A network of computers checks and confirms each transaction, ensuring transparency and security.

COMMON USES

People use cryptocurrencies to shop online, invest, or raise funds through ICOs (Initial Coin Offerings).

FAMOUS CRYPTOS

Well-known digital currencies include Bitcoin, Ethereum, and Dogecoin, each serving different purposes.

FUN FACT

THE TOTAL NUMBER OF BITCOINS IS CAPPED AT 21 MILLION, MAKING IT A LIMITED DIGITAL RESOURCE!

How do we stay safe online?

Cybersecurity defends computers, networks, and personal data from hackers, keeping online activities secure and private.

PROTECTING YOUR INFORMATION

Data is scrambled with encryption, firewalls keep hackers out, and strong passwords guard your accounts.

WHY CYBER SAFETY MATTERS

It stops hackers from stealing private or financial information during online activities.

SMART ONLINE HABITS

Create strong passwords, keep personal info private, and avoid clicking on unknown links.

FUN FACT

THE FIRST COMPUTER VIRUS, CALLED "CREEPER", APPEARED IN THE EARLY 1970S—LONG BEFORE MODERN CYBERSECURITY TOOLS!

How does edge computing work?

Edge computing is a technology that processes data close to its source, making it faster and reducing the need for distant servers.

HOW IT FUNCTIONS

Data is handled nearby, on local devices or close servers, instead of travelling to distant data centres.

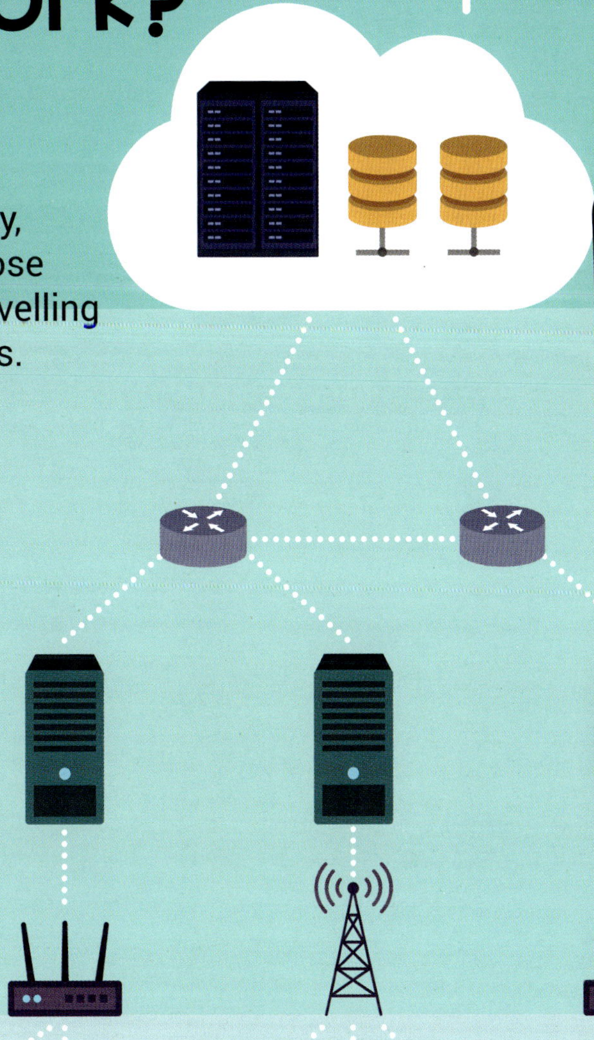

BRAIN BUZZ

- Where is edge computing used?
- Why is edge computing faster?
- Does edge computing save bandwidth?

REAL-LIFE USES

Edge computing powers smart home devices, fitness wearables, and self-driving cars.

WHY IT'S HELPFUL

It offers quicker responses, saves internet bandwidth, and keeps data more secure.

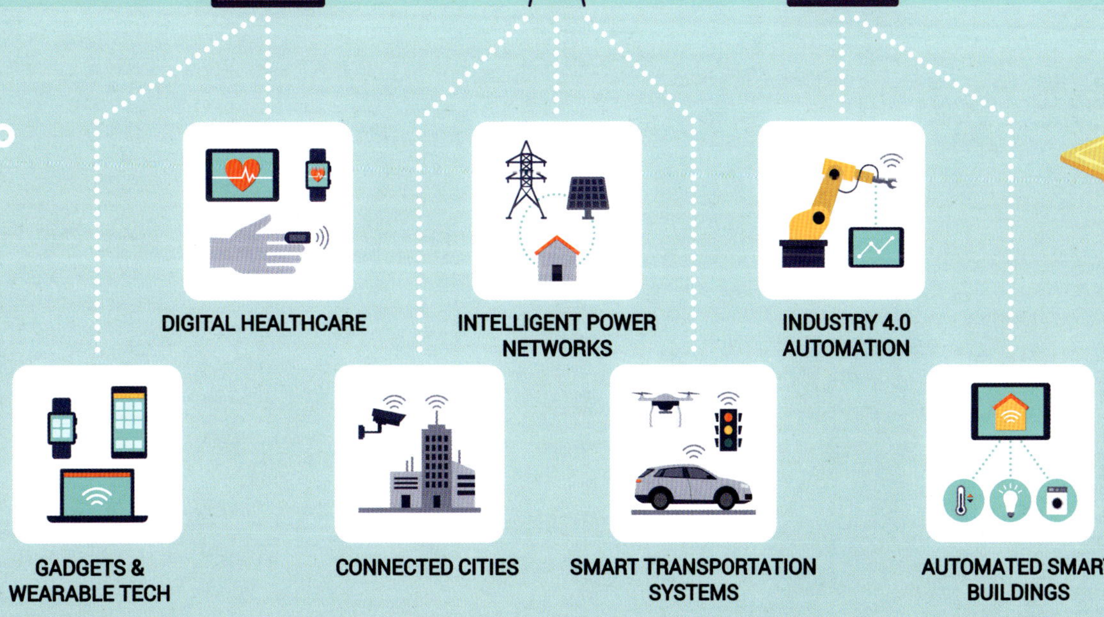

What are programmable machines?

Programmable machines, called robots, are designed to perform tasks like assembling cars, cleaning floors, or exploring space!

HOW ROBOTS ARE USEFUL

Robots assist in surgeries, explore distant planets, and help with chores at home.

DIFFERENT KINDS OF ROBOTS

Some are human-like, while others are simple machines, such as robotic arms in factories.

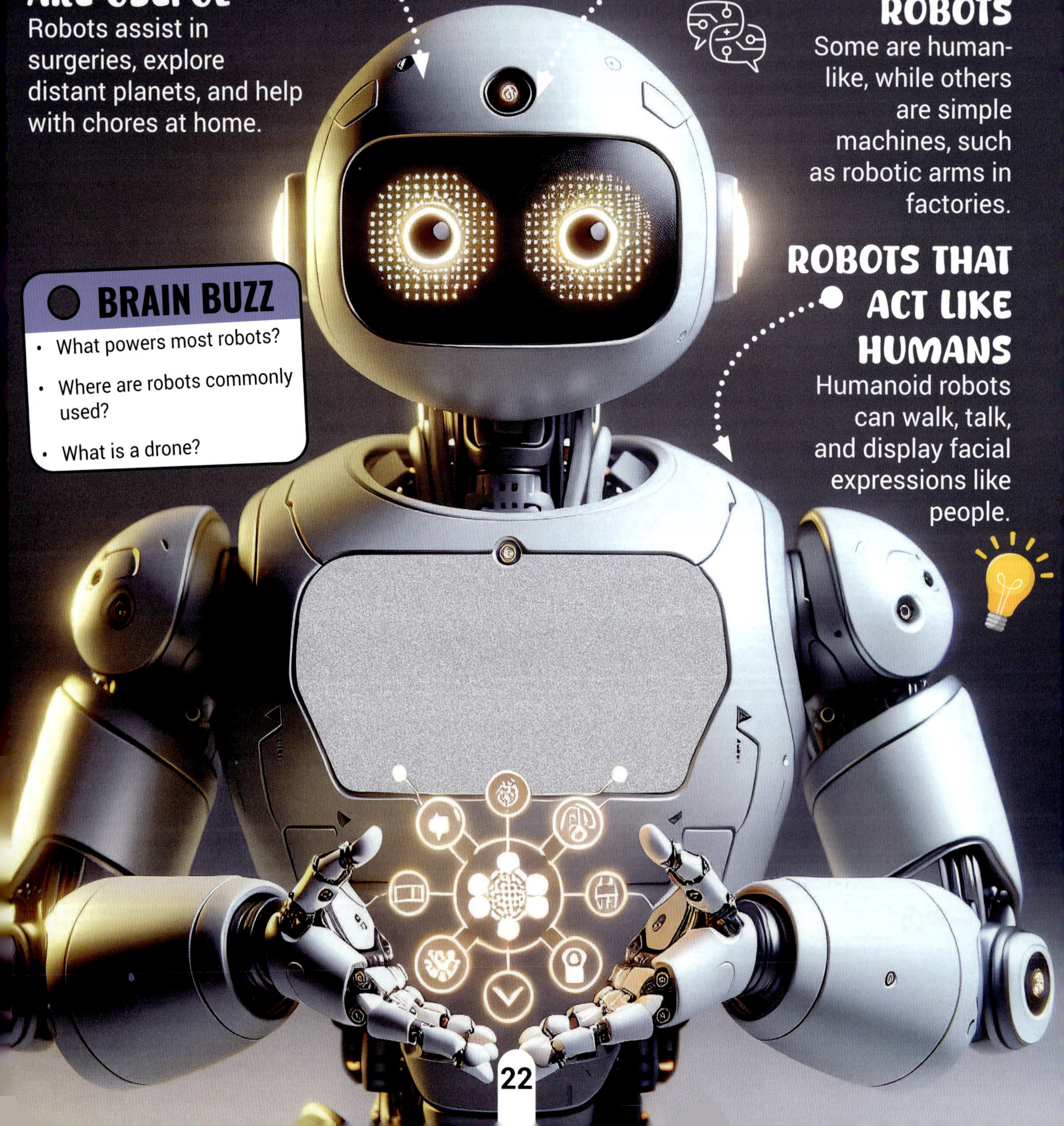

BRAIN BUZZ

- What powers most robots?
- Where are robots commonly used?
- What is a drone?

ROBOTS THAT ACT LIKE HUMANS

Humanoid robots can walk, talk, and display facial expressions like people.

What are self-operating robots?

Self-operating robots are autonomous machines. They can carry out tasks independently, without needing human control. Examples include robotic vacuum cleaners and self-driving cars.

HOW THEY WORK

Autonomous robots work independently, using sensors and AI to complete tasks without human input.

REAL-WORLD EXAMPLES

Drones, robotic floor cleaners, delivery bots, and factory machines.

HOW THEY HELP

They help with cleaning, package delivery, and automated manufacturing.

FUN FACT

AUTONOMOUS UNDERWATER ROBOTS EXPLORE THE DEEPEST PARTS OF THE OCEAN WHERE HUMANS CAN'T GO.

What is an autonomous vehicle?

An autonomous vehicle drives on its own, using advanced sensors and AI instead of a human driver.

BRAIN BUZZ

- What powers self-driving cars?
- Where are self-driving cars tested?
- Can they work at night?

HOW THEY DRIVE THEMSELVES

With a combination of cameras, radar, sensors, and AI, these vehicles sense their environment and make safe driving choices.

DESIGNED FOR SAFETY

They help reduce accidents by detecting dangers early and responding faster than human drivers.

AUTONOMY STAGES

From simple driving aids to completely self-driving cars, autonomy comes in various levels.

What are Self-Operating Ships?

Self-operating ships are vessels that use AI and sensors to sail and perform tasks without needing people onboard.

SMART NAVIGATION

Autonomous ships use AI to read sea conditions and avoid hazards along the route.

PRACTICAL USES

These vessels carry cargo, study ocean life, and perform environmental monitoring.

GREENER SHIPPING

They help reduce pollution by using energy-efficient routes and eco-friendly technology.

WHY THEY MATTER

They cut down expenses, improve safety, and help reduce fuel consumption.

SMART HULLS

Their sleek lower design helps them glide smoothly, saving energy and cutting fuel use.

FUN FACT

SOME AUTONOMOUS SHIPS USE UNDERWATER DRONES TO INSPECT THEIR HULLS AND EXPLORE DEEP-SEA AREAS!

How do drones stay in the air?

Drones stay airborne by using spinning propellers, guided by sensors and remote controls. They can deliver packages, take photos, and more!

LIFT-OFF AND MOVEMENT

Propellers push air down, letting drones lift off, stay steady, and zip around smoothly.

STEERING THE FLIGHT

Controllers or apps direct drones, while smart drones can follow GPS routes automatically.

DRONE JOBS

From delivering goods and snapping photos to rescuing people and studying animals, drones are super handy!

FUN FACT

DRONES COME IN ALL SIZES—SOME FIT IN YOUR PALM, WHILE OTHERS ARE AS BIG AS SMALL PLANES AND USED IN THE MILITARY.

What are robotic exoskeleton suits?

Robotic exoskeleton suits are wearable machines that boost a person's strength and movement. They help people recover from injuries and assist workers with heavy tasks.

HOW IT FUNCTIONS

Exoskeletons have sensors that track body movements and motors that offer extra support, allowing smoother, natural motions.

HEALTHCARE APPLICATIONS

They help people with paralysis walk again and support stroke recovery by improving mobility during therapy.

WORKPLACE APPLICATIONS

Exoskeletons assist workers by reducing tiredness and lowering the risk of injuries when lifting or handling heavy loads.

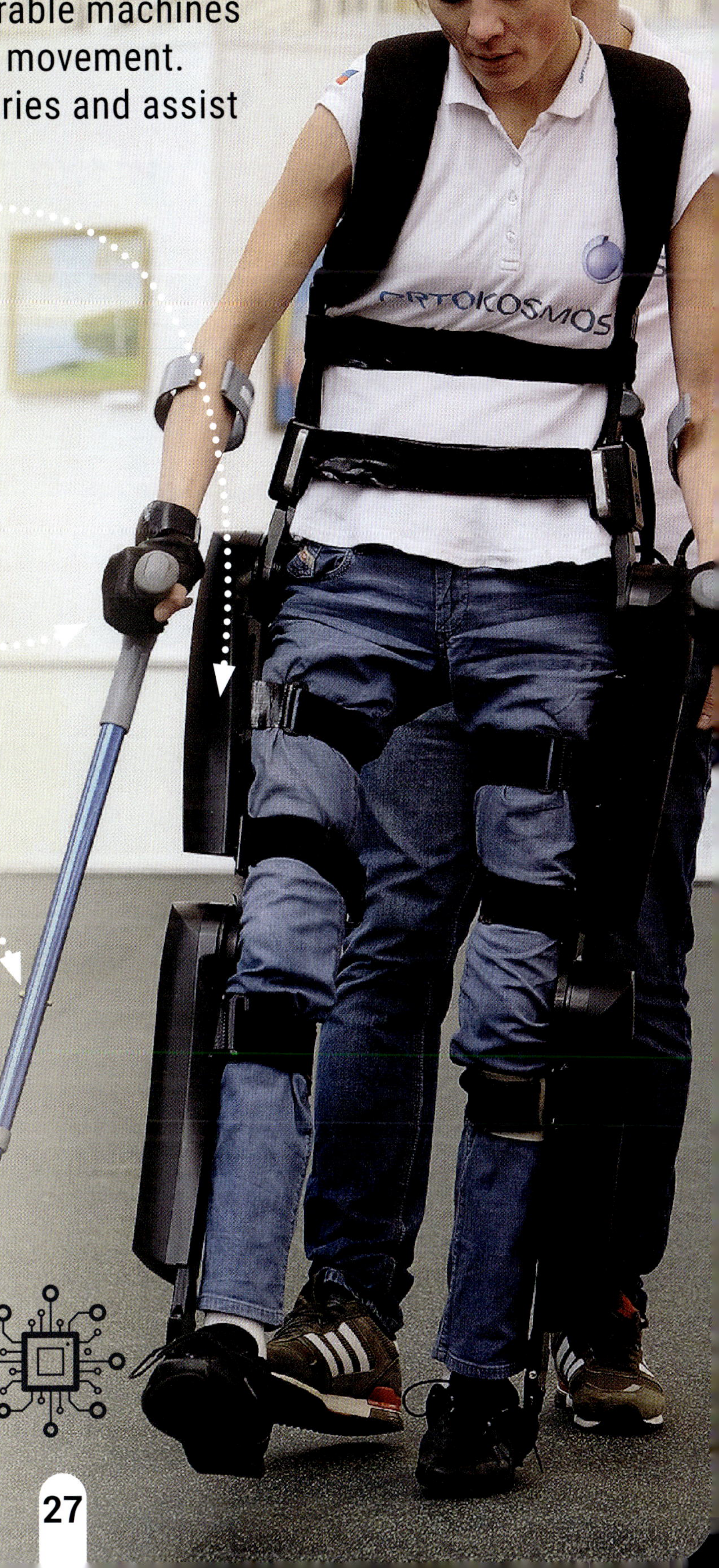

FUN FACT

SOME MODERN EXOSKELETONS ARE POWERED BY AI, ALLOWING THEM TO ADAPT IN REAL-TIME TO A PERSON'S MOVEMENTS FOR SMOOTHER SUPPORT!

How is robotics used in healthcare?

Robotic systems help doctors perform surgeries, diagnose illnesses, and improve patient care with high accuracy and efficiency.

ROBOTIC SURGERY

Advanced systems like the da Vinci robot perform precise, minimally invasive surgeries, helping patients heal faster.

REHABILITATION ROBOTS

These assist patients in physical therapy, helping them regain strength and mobility.

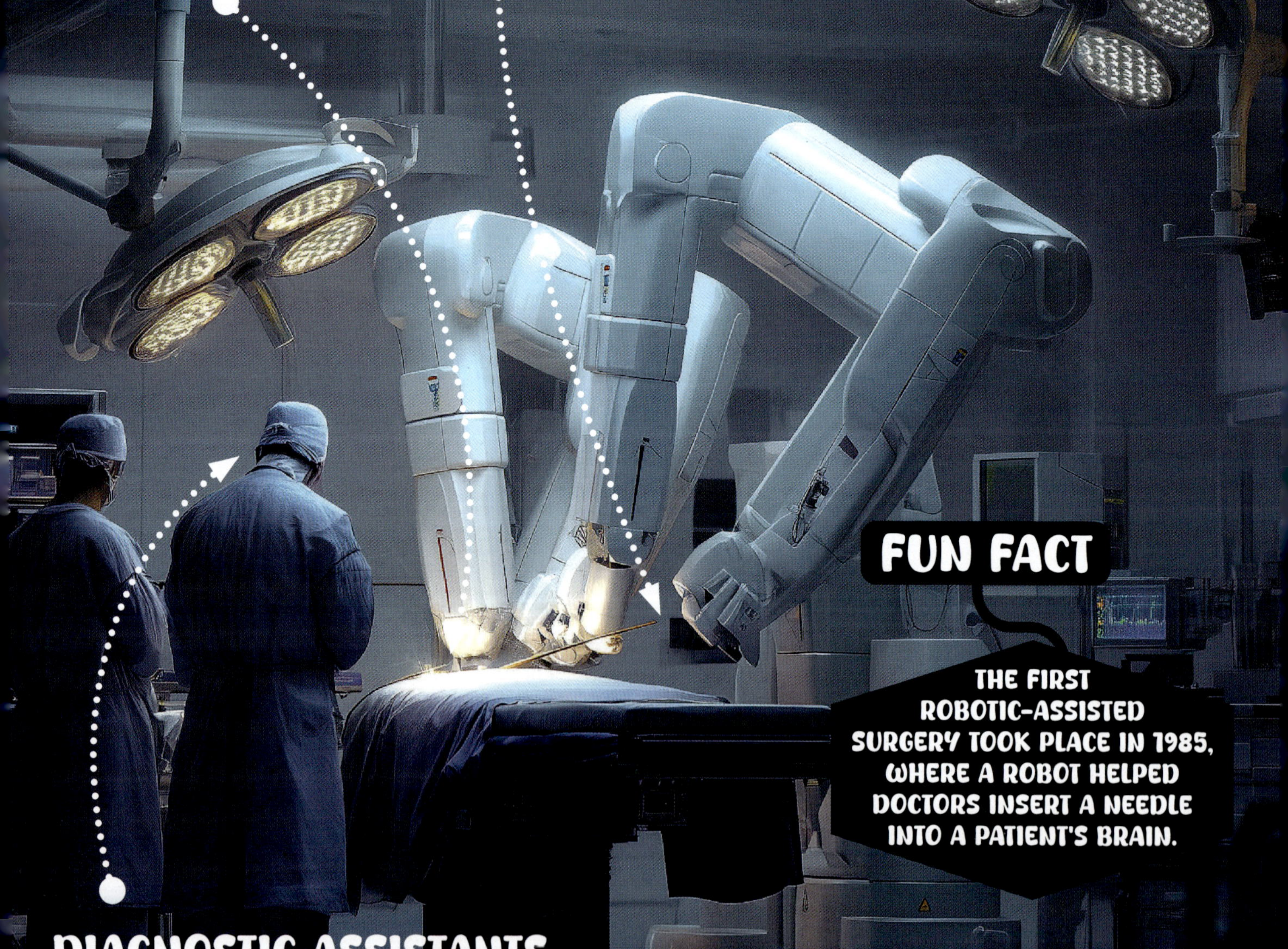

FUN FACT

THE FIRST ROBOTIC-ASSISTED SURGERY TOOK PLACE IN 1985, WHERE A ROBOT HELPED DOCTORS INSERT A NEEDLE INTO A PATIENT'S BRAIN.

DIAGNOSTIC ASSISTANTS

AI-powered robots scan X-rays and MRIs to spot diseases early and assist doctors in making accurate diagnoses.

What does Virtual Reality (VR) allow you to experience?

Virtual Reality lets you enter a computer-made 3D world using special headsets, making you feel like you're really inside a game or scene.

WHERE VR IS USED

VR helps with entertainment, education, and professional training—making learning and fun more exciting.

EXPLORE NEW WORLDS

VR lets you explore amazing places, from ancient cities to outer space, without leaving home.

VR TECHNOLOGY

VR goggles have screens and motion sensors that create a 3D world, making it feel like you're really there.

FUN FACT

THE WORLD'S FIRST 3D-PRINTED CAR WAS MADE IN JUST 44 HOURS!

How does Augmented Reality (AR) work?

Augmented Reality adds digital images and information to the real world. It works through smartphones, tablets, or AR glasses that display virtual objects alongside what you see in real life.

SEEING THE REAL + VIRTUAL

AR blends real-world views with computer-generated images, making your surroundings more interactive.

FUN AND GAMES

From catching virtual creatures to trying funny face filters, AR adds a playful twist to everyday experiences.

BRAIN BUZZ

- What devices use AR?
- Who uses AR?
- Can AR help learning?
- Is AR different from VR?

HELPFUL IN DAILY LIFE

Use AR to test how shoes look on your feet, get directions with arrows on your screen, or explore planets in 3D.

How is augmented reality used in education?

Augmented reality makes learning fun by adding 3D models, animations, and facts to real-world lessons, helping students understand subjects better.

INTERACTIVE LEARNING

AR brings textbooks to life with 3D visuals and interactive activities.

COOL EXAMPLES

With AR, kids can explore planets, dissect virtual animals, or step into important moments from history.

LEARNING MADE FUN

AR makes lessons more exciting, helping students stay focused and learn better.

FUN FACT

WITH AR, STUDENTS CAN WALK THROUGH ANCIENT CITIES AND EVEN MEET HISTORICAL FIGURES VIRTUALLY.

How does hologram technology create 3D images?

Hologram technology uses light to project 3D images that seem to float in mid-air. These lifelike images are used in entertainment, education, and other fields to amaze and inform people.

FUN FACT

HOLOGRAMS HAVE BEEN USED TO BRING FAMOUS HISTORICAL FIGURES LIKE EINSTEIN AND CLEOPATRA TO LIFE IN MUSEUMS AND EXHIBITIONS!

EVERYDAY USES

Holograms are used in live concerts with virtual performers, interactive museum displays, and advanced medical training simulations.

HOW IT WORKS

Lasers split light beams to create patterns that, when combined, display 3D images that can be seen from different angles.

WHAT'S NEXT?

In the future, holograms could replace flat screens, making 3D video calls, gaming, and virtual shopping a normal part of life.

What is the purpose of a 3D printer?

A 3D printer is a tool for creating three-dimensional items by stacking layers of material guided by computer models.

STARRY SPECTACLE

This massive group of around 3,000 stars shines like a cosmic firework show! It's called Westerlund 2, and it lies in our own Milky Way galaxy.

CREATIONS WITH 3D PRINTERS

From toys and tools to artificial bones and even houses, 3D printers are used to create all kinds of amazing things!

WHAT 3D PRINTERS USE

3D printers work with different materials like plastic, metal, and even chocolate to build their objects, layer by layer.

FUN FACT

SCIENTISTS ARE USING 3D PRINTERS TO CREATE HUMAN ORGANS, LIKE EARS AND SKIN, FOR MEDICAL RESEARCH!

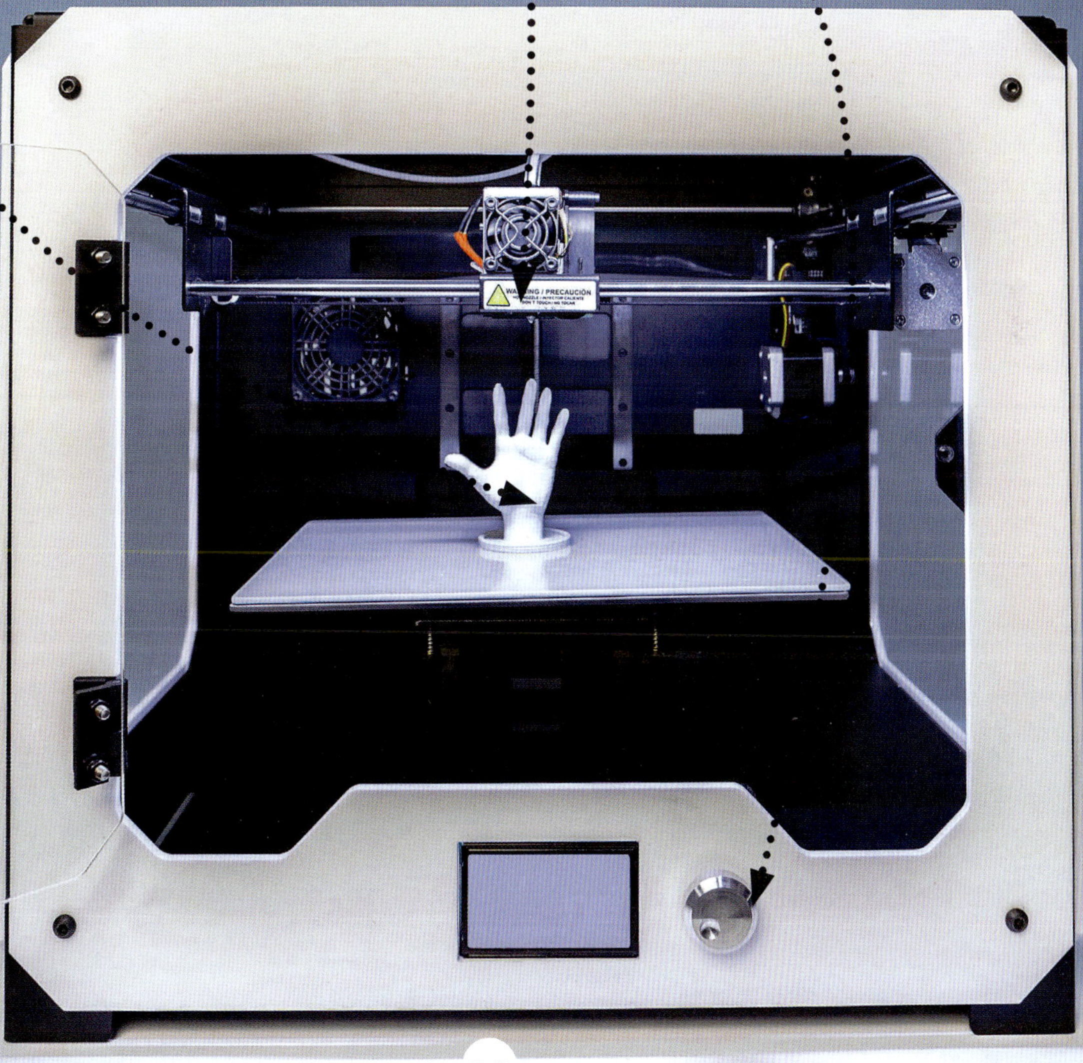

What is the process of creating living tissues and organs using 3D printing technology?

Bioprinting is a process that employs 3D printing technology to produce living tissues and organs, holding the potential to revolutionize medicine and healthcare.

HOW IT FUNCTIONS

Cells are utilized as "ink" to print layers that form various tissues, such as skin, bones, or even organs.

POTENTIAL USES

Bioprinting aids in creating skin for burn victims and may eventually address the shortage of organ donors.

OBSTACLES

Creating fully functional organs remains a challenging task, but researchers are making notable advancements.

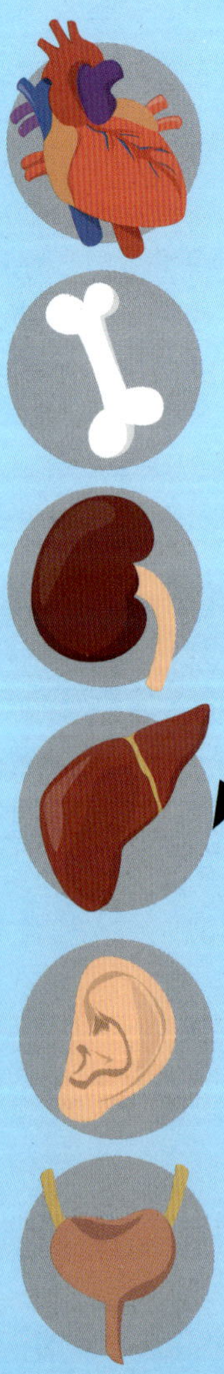

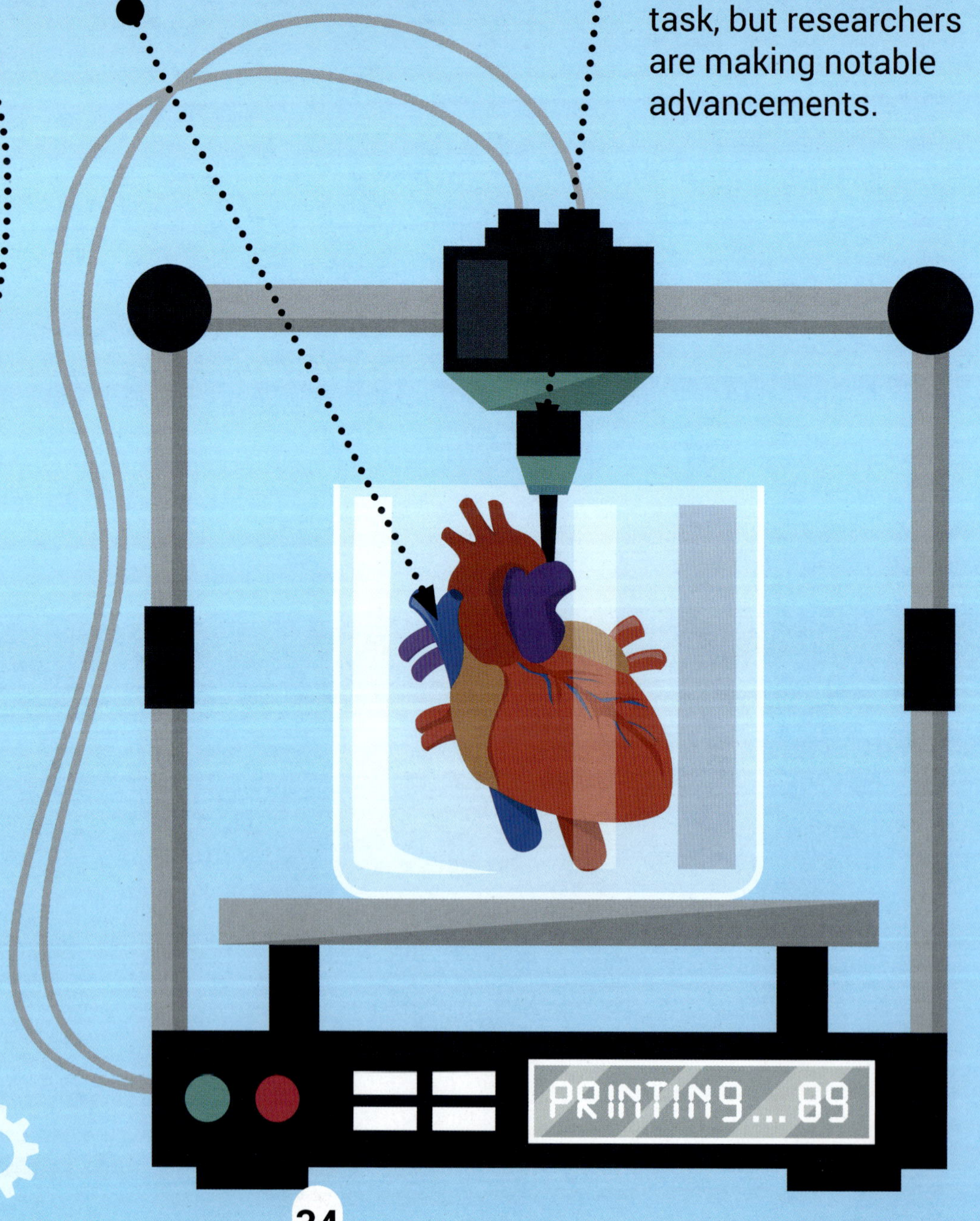

What is the role of biometric technologies in identifying individuals?

Biometric technologies identify individuals by analyzing unique physical characteristics, such as fingerprints, facial features, or voice patterns.

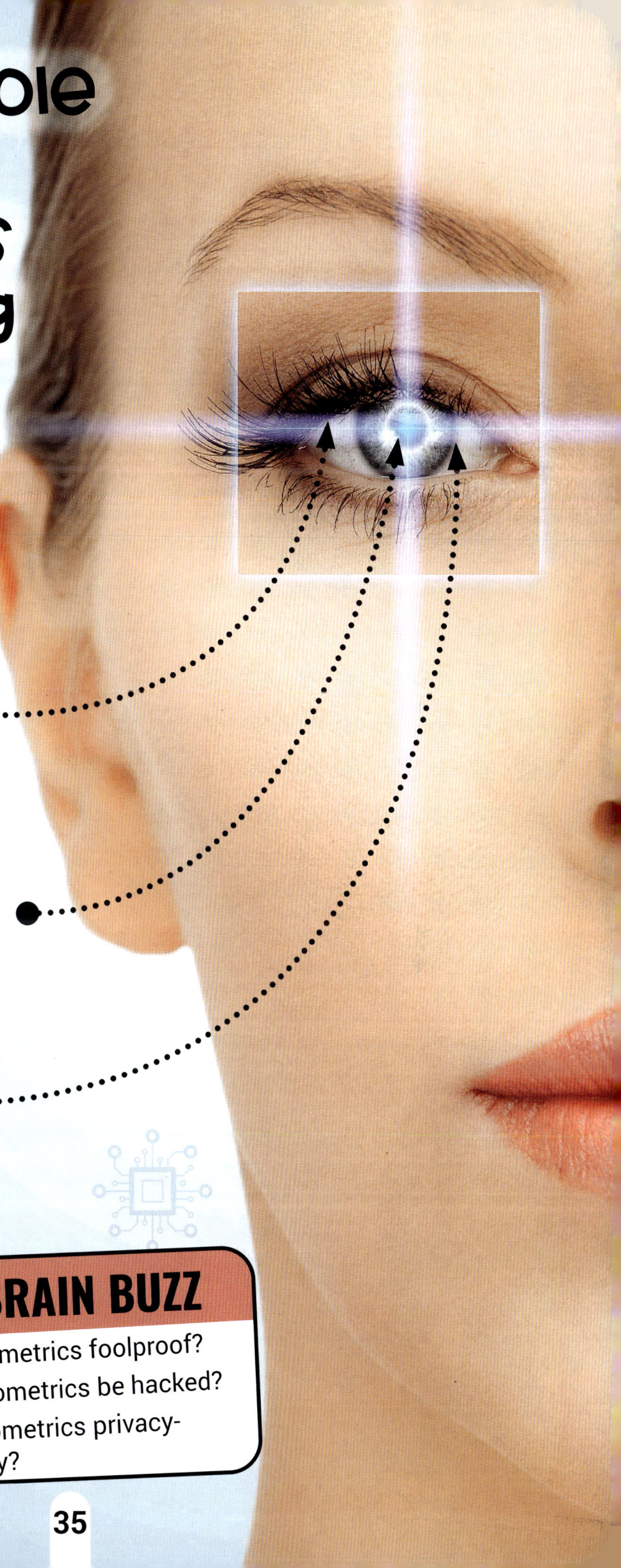

HOW IT OPERATES

Biometric devices scan unique features like fingerprints or faces and compare them to stored data for identification or security purposes.

COMMON APPLICATIONS

Used for unlocking smartphones, protecting bank accounts, or granting access to high-security areas.

EVERYDAY BENEFITS

Biometric methods offer quicker and more secure authentication than traditional passwords, as they are exclusive to each individual.

BRAIN BUZZ

- Are biometrics foolproof?
- Can biometrics be hacked?
- Are biometrics privacy-friendly?

What are the man-made devices that replace or support natural organs?

Artificial organs are devices created to replace or assist the function of natural organs, such as artificial hearts or kidneys.

MEDICAL ADVANCEMENTS

Artificial organs help save lives and enhance patients' quality of life.

FUNCTIONALITY

These devices replicate the functions of real organs to maintain health.

NOTABLE EXAMPLES

Artificial hearts pump blood, while dialysis machines perform the blood-cleaning function of kidneys.

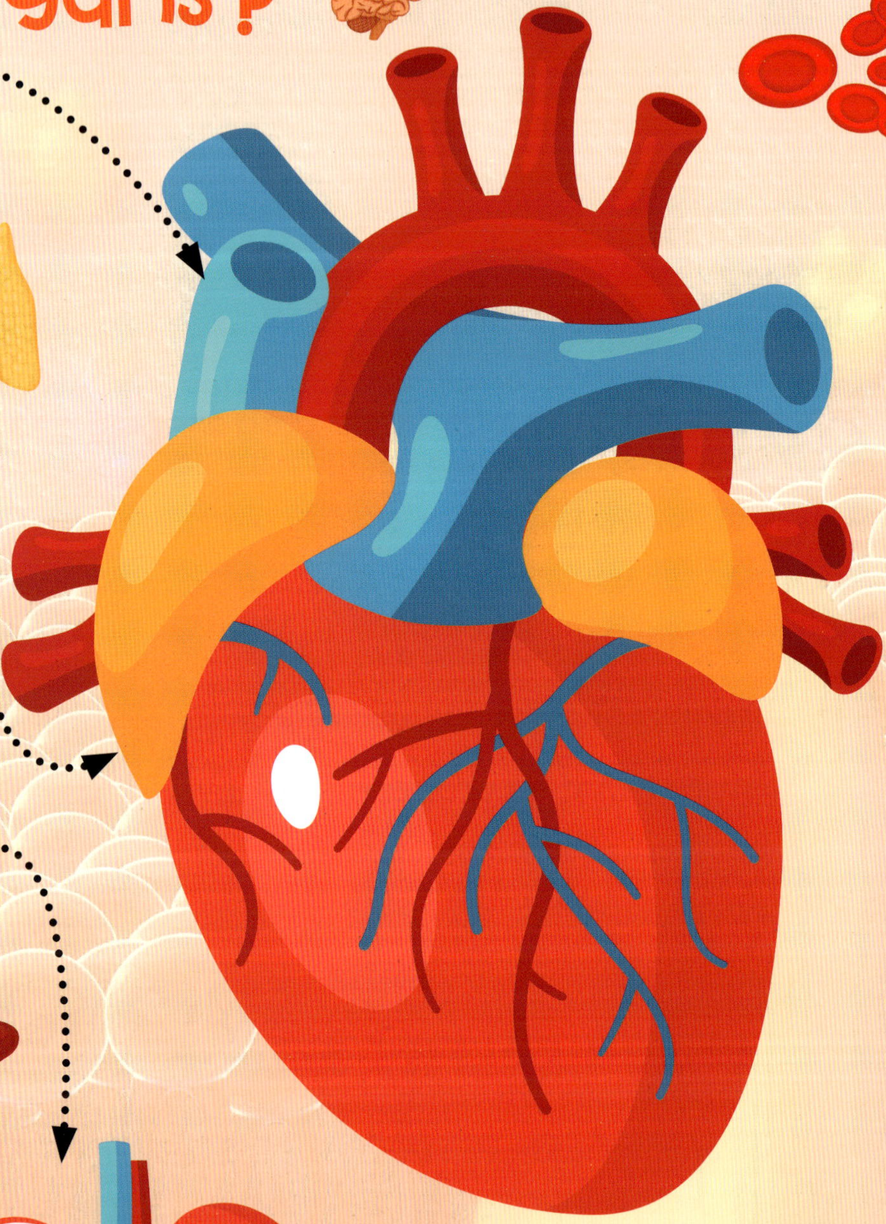

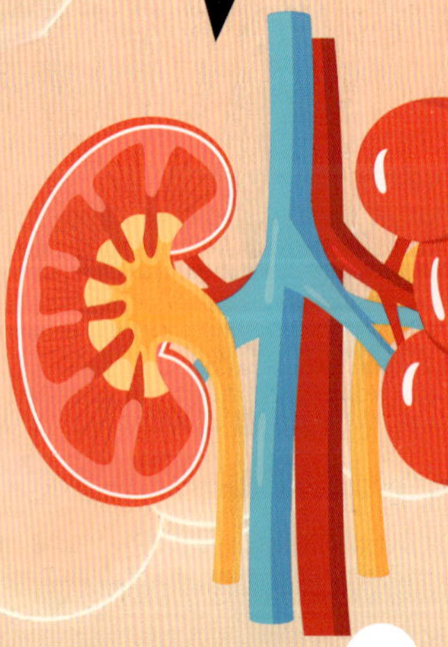

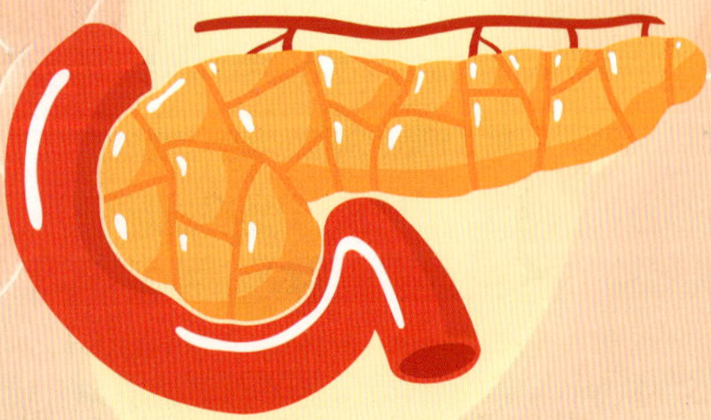

FUN FACT

THE WORLD'S FIRST SUCCESSFUL KIDNEY TRANSPLANT TOOK PLACE IN 1954.

What does genetic engineering involve in altering an organism?

Genetic engineering alters an organism's DNA to introduce new traits, enhancing its strength, health, or productivity.

ETHICAL CONSIDERATIONS

Though offering great benefits, genetic engineering raises concerns about over-manipulating nature.

PRACTICAL USES

It is applied to develop pest-resistant crops, produce life-saving medicines, and study genetic disorders.

HOW IT FUNCTIONS

Techniques such as CRISPR enable precise gene alterations, allowing scientists to enhance or repair DNA.

BRAIN BUZZ

- Can genetic engineering cure diseases?
- What is CRISPR?
- Are genetically modified crops harmful?

What do biohacking technologies do to improve the human body?

Biohacking uses science and technology to enhance the human body through wearable devices, implantable tech, or changes in lifestyle.

HEALTH ADVANTAGES

Biohacking enables the tracking of fitness, improvement of sleep quality, optimization of diets, and stress reduction through personalized data.

BIOHACKING EXAMPLES

Biohackers use smart pills for health monitoring or implant microchips to replace keys, cards, and IDs.

ETHICAL CONCERNS

There are concerns that enhancing the body with technology may cause over-dependence or increase inequality between those with and without access.

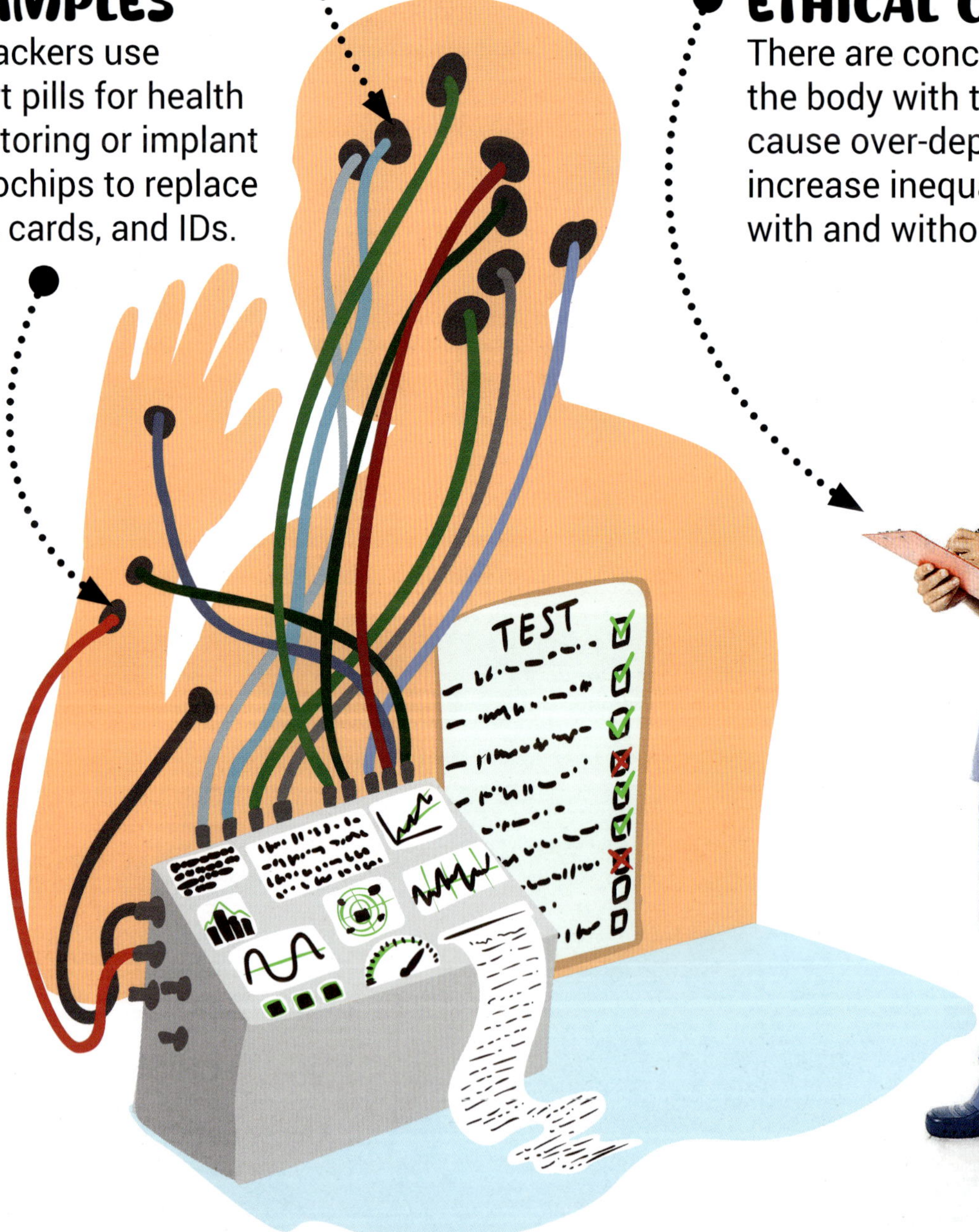

What are nanobots and how do they function?

Nanobots are minuscule robots, often smaller than a cell, that carry out tasks at a microscopic level, particularly in medicine and research.

FUTURE POSSIBILITIES

Nanobots may help clean polluted water or construct materials at the atomic scale.

WHAT GUIDES FUNCTION

Nanobots are guided by magnetic fields, light, or other signals to perform precise tasks.

MEDICAL APPLICATIONS

They can deliver medicine directly to cancer cells or repair tissues at a microscopic level.

FUN FACT

NANOBOTS COULD ONE DAY BE USED TO DETECT DISEASES IN THE BODY BEFORE SYMPTOMS APPEAR.

What does nanotechnology involve in creating small and powerful tools?

Nanotechnology focuses on manipulating materials at the atomic and molecular scale to develop extremely small and powerful tools.

HOW IT FUNCTIONS

Scientists work with particles smaller than a human hair to create materials with special properties.

USES AND APPLICATIONS

Nanotechnology is applied in medicine, electronics, and to create stronger, lighter materials.

PRACTICAL EXAMPLES

In cancer treatment, nanoparticles deliver drugs directly to tumors, reducing side effects.

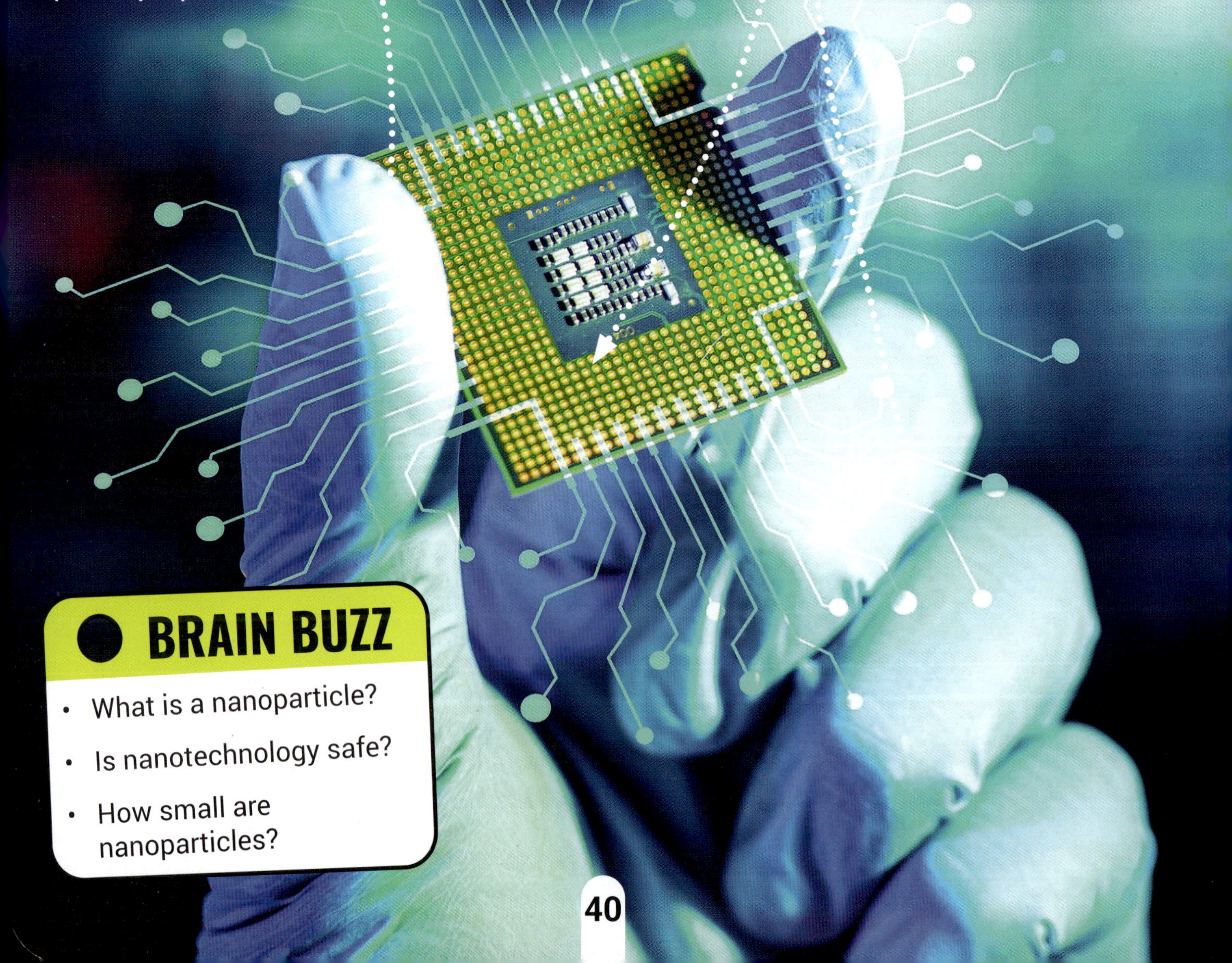

BRAIN BUZZ

- What is a nanoparticle?
- Is nanotechnology safe?
- How small are nanoparticles?

What types of smart devices are considered wearable technologies?

Wearable technologies are smart devices that can be worn, such as fitness trackers, smartwatches, and smart glasses.

HOW THEY FUNCTION

These devices use sensors to monitor your activity, health, or location and transmit the data to an app or other device.

COMMON EXAMPLES

Fitness bands track steps, smartwatches manage calls, and AR glasses display information directly in your view.

HEALTH ADVANTAGES

Wearables monitor heart rate, track sleep patterns, and detect stress levels.

FUN FACT

THE FIRST SMARTWATCHES WERE INTRODUCED IN THE 1990S, LONG BEFORE TODAY'S VERSIONS.

How do smart wearables assist in healthcare?

Smart wearables, like fitness trackers and smartwatches, monitor health and activity, helping people maintain fitness and detect health issues early.

FUN FACT

SOME SMARTWATCHES CAN MONITOR ECGS TO DETECT HEART CONDITIONS LIKE ATRIAL FIBRILLATION.

HEALTH ADVANTAGES

Detect irregular heartbeats, monitor blood oxygen levels, and track fitness progress.

HOW THEY FUNCTION

Sensors in wearables track steps, heart rate, and sleep patterns, transmitting data to apps for analysis.

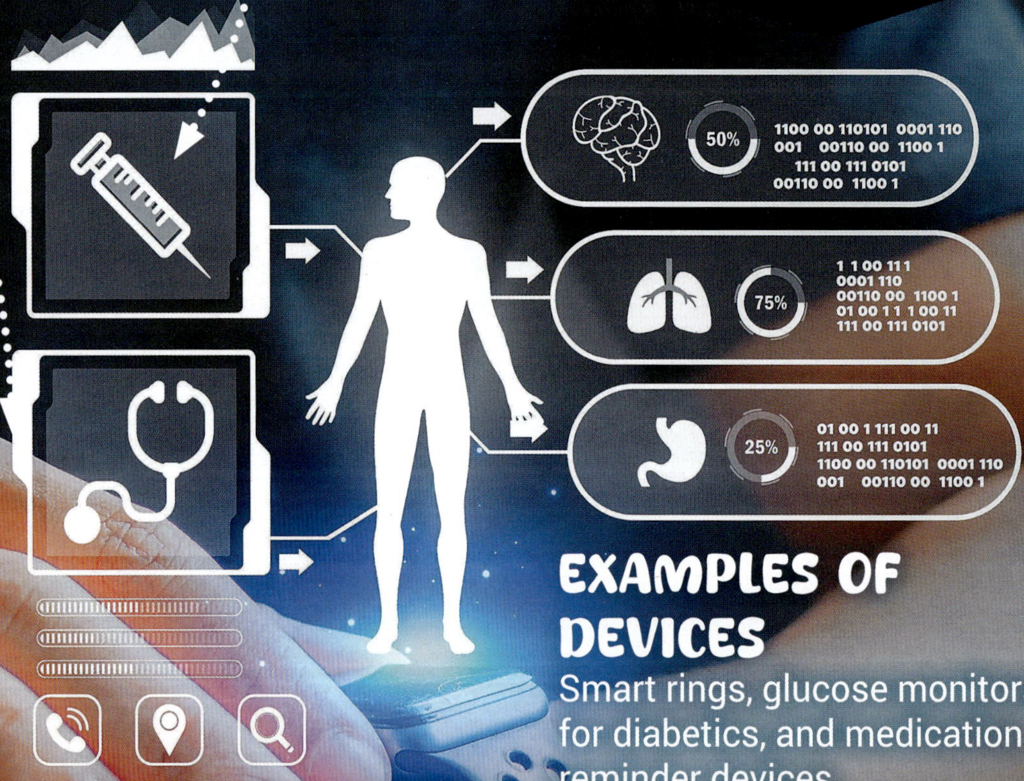

EXAMPLES OF DEVICES

Smart rings, glucose monitors for diabetics, and medication reminder devices.

What does smart home technology do to improve homes?

Smart home technology uses devices like smart speakers, thermostats, and lights to enhance convenience and efficiency in homes.

FUN FACT

SOME SMART HOMES CAN SEND ALERTS IF UNUSUAL ACTIVITY IS DETECTED, LIKE AN OPEN DOOR OR WINDOW.

ENERGY SAVINGS

Smart homes reduce energy consumption by automating lights, appliances, and heating systems.

HOW IT OPERATES

Devices connect to Wi-Fi and can be managed through apps or voice commands.

COMMON EXAMPLES

Smart thermostats adjust temperature, smart lights change colour, and video doorbells improve security.

How do smart cities enhance urban living?

Smart cities utilize advanced technologies like sensors, data analysis, and AI to manage resources efficiently and improve the quality of life.

HOW IT FUNCTIONS

Sensors in roads, buildings, and utilities collect real-time data to optimize traffic flow, water use, and energy management.

KEY EXAMPLES

Automated waste collection, traffic signals that adjust to congestion, and energy-saving lighting systems.

ADVANTAGES

Less waste, cleaner air, improved public transport, and faster emergency responses.

FUN FACT

CITIES LIKE BARCELONA USE SENSORS TO MONITOR AIR QUALITY AND REDUCE POLLUTION.

What is the purpose of a digital twin?

A digital twin is a virtual representation of a physical object, process, or system used to simulate and analyze its performance.

HOW IT FUNCTIONS

Sensors on physical objects send data to computers, creating digital replicas that reflect the real-world items.

APPLICATIONS

Engineers test prototypes, factories enhance production efficiency, and cities manage traffic flow using digital twins.

REAL-WORLD EXAMPLES

Digital twins monitor bridges, predict machine malfunctions, and improve healthcare devices.

FUN FACT

DIGITAL TWINS HELP MONITOR AND PREDICT THE PERFORMANCE OF SATELLITES IN SPACE.

How does renewable energy technology generate electricity?

Renewable energy technology harnesses natural resources like sunlight, wind, and water to produce electricity in an environmentally friendly manner.

WIND ENERGY

Large blades capture wind to generate electricity, typically installed in fields or offshore.

FUN FACT

WIND TURBINES CAN PRODUCE ELECTRICITY EVEN AT LOW WIND SPEEDS, MAKING THEM EFFICIENT IN MANY AREAS.

WATER POWER

Flowing water from dams turns turbines to produce reliable and clean energy.

SOLAR POWER

Solar panels absorb sunlight and convert it into electricity to power homes, schools, and vehicles.

BRAIN BUZZ

- What is the most common renewable energy source?
- What is the lifespan of a wind turbine?
- Is hydropower environmentally friendly?

What are renewable fuels made from?

Renewable fuels are environmentally friendly energy sources derived from naturally replenishable materials such as plants, algae, or organic waste.

TYPES OF RENEWABLE FUELS

Biofuels from corn, algae-based energy, and biodiesel from used cooking oil.

APPLICATIONS

Used in vehicles, planes, and industries to reduce carbon emissions.

ENVIRONMENTAL BENEFITS

Renewable fuels generate much less pollution, aiding in climate change mitigation.

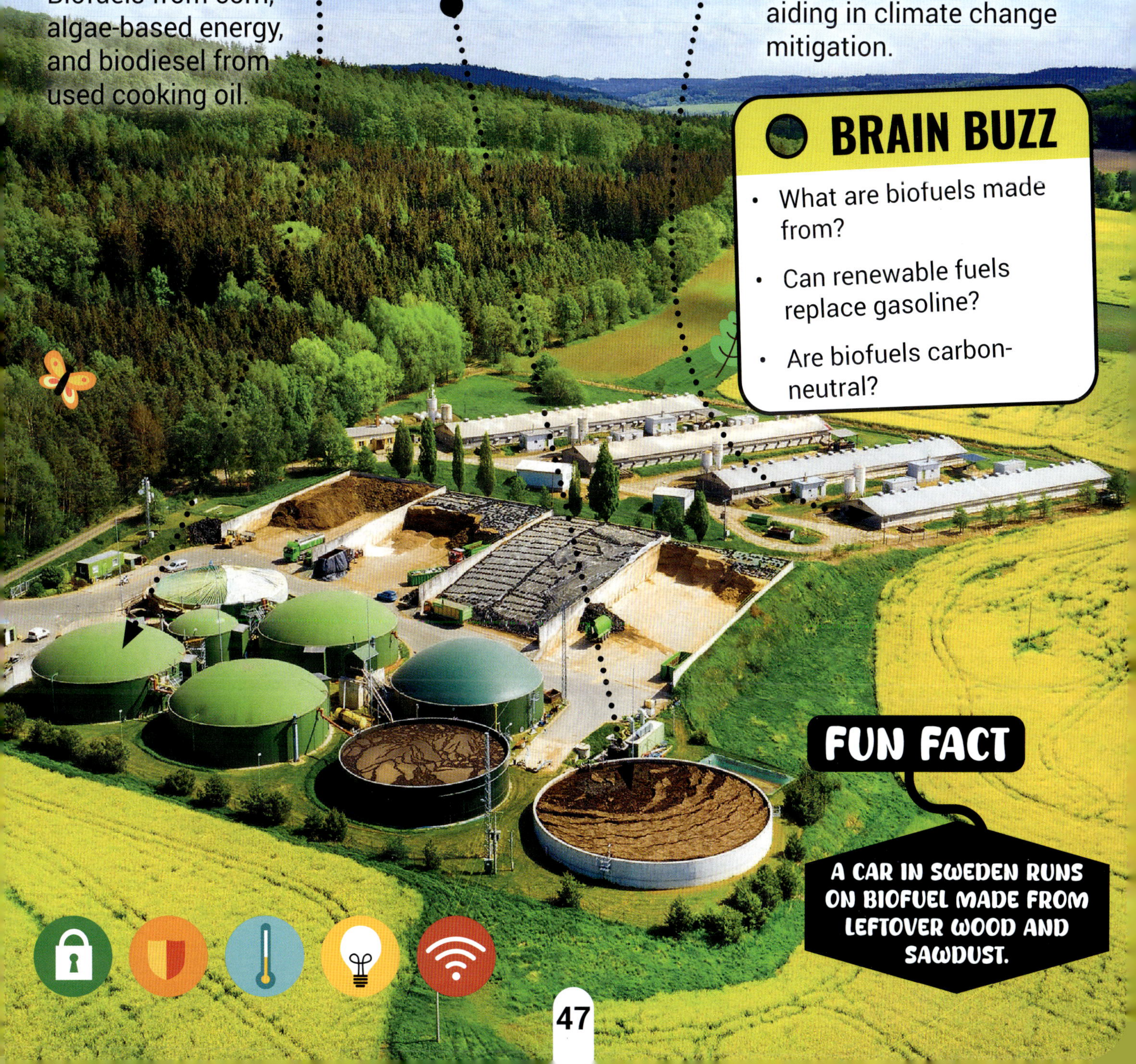

BRAIN BUZZ

- What are biofuels made from?
- Can renewable fuels replace gasoline?
- Are biofuels carbon-neutral?

FUN FACT

A CAR IN SWEDEN RUNS ON BIOFUEL MADE FROM LEFTOVER WOOD AND SAWDUST.

What are renewable materials made of?

Renewable materials are sustainable resources that naturally regenerate, such as bamboo, cork, and bioplastics.

EXAMPLES

Bamboo is fast-growing and used for furniture, while bioplastics are plant-based alternatives to petroleum plastics.

BENEFITS

Renewable materials help reduce dependency on non-renewable resources, are often biodegradable, and have a lower environmental impact.

APPLICATIONS

These materials are used in packaging, fashion, and construction to support sustainable practices.

FUN FACT

BAMBOO FABRIC IS NATURALLY ANTIBACTERIAL, MAKING IT PERFECT FOR ECO-FRIENDLY CLOTHING.

What is sustainable building design?

Sustainable building design uses eco-friendly materials and energy-efficient methods to create structures that minimize environmental impact.

HOW IT WORKS

Designs incorporate solar power, green roofing, and energy-saving features to reduce environmental harm.

EXAMPLES

Buildings with wind turbines or homes using recycled materials for construction.

FUTURE VISION

The goal is to build self-sustaining structures that run entirely on renewable energy.

FUN FACT

"THE EDGE" IN AMSTERDAM IS SO ENERGY-EFFICIENT THAT IT PRODUCES MORE ENERGY THAN IT CONSUMES!

What is Carbon Capture Technology Used For?

Carbon capture technology captures carbon dioxide emissions from factories and power plants, stopping them from being released into the atmosphere.

TECHNOLOGY IN ACTION

CO_2 is filtered, compressed, and either stored underground or repurposed in products like fuel.

POSITIVE IMPACT

Minimizes greenhouse gases, contributing to the fight against climate change.

INDUSTRY ADOPTION

Employed in industries such as cement manufacturing and natural gas extraction.

BRAIN BUZZ

- What gases are captured?
- Can carbon be reused?
- Is carbon capture effective?

What is space tech?

Space tech refers to devices and systems like rockets, satellites, and telescopes that are created for exploring and studying space.

SATELLITE FUNCTIONS

Satellites enable worldwide communication, track weather patterns, and assist in disaster recovery efforts.

EXPLORATION BREAKTHROUGHS

Reusable rockets, such as SpaceX's Falcon 9, are making space exploration more affordable.

MARS EXPLORATION

Rovers like Perseverance gather valuable samples and data from distant planets, including Mars.

FUN FACT

THE INTERNATIONAL SPACE STATION (ISS) COMPLETES 16 ORBITS AROUND EARTH EVERY DAY, ALLOWING ASTRONAUTS TO WITNESS 16 SUNRISES AND SUNSETS.

What is space travel for tourists?

Space travel for tourists allows regular people to venture beyond Earth, enjoy weightlessness, and witness stunning views of our planet.

PRIVATE SPACE TRAVEL

Private firms like SpaceX and Blue Origin launch rockets to take passengers on brief space journeys.

THE EXPERIENCE

Travellers enjoy weightlessness, view Earth from space, and safely return to Earth after the trip.

LOOKING AHEAD

Space hotels and lunar or Martian stays might become possible in the near future.

FUN FACT

IN 2021, SPACEX'S INSPIRATION4 MISSION TOOK THE FIRST ALL-CIVILIAN CREW ON A JOURNEY TO SPACE!

What is a brain-computer connection system?

A brain-computer connection system is an advanced technology that allows direct interaction between the brain and computers. It uses special sensors to detect brain signals and turn them into digital commands.

PROCESS OVERVIEW

Brain-computer interfaces (BCIs) use electrodes placed on the scalp or inside the brain to detect electrical signals. These signals are processed and converted into digital instructions to control various devices..

REAL-WORLD USES

BCIs assist people with disabilities by enabling control of prosthetic limbs, typing through thought, and non-verbal communication.

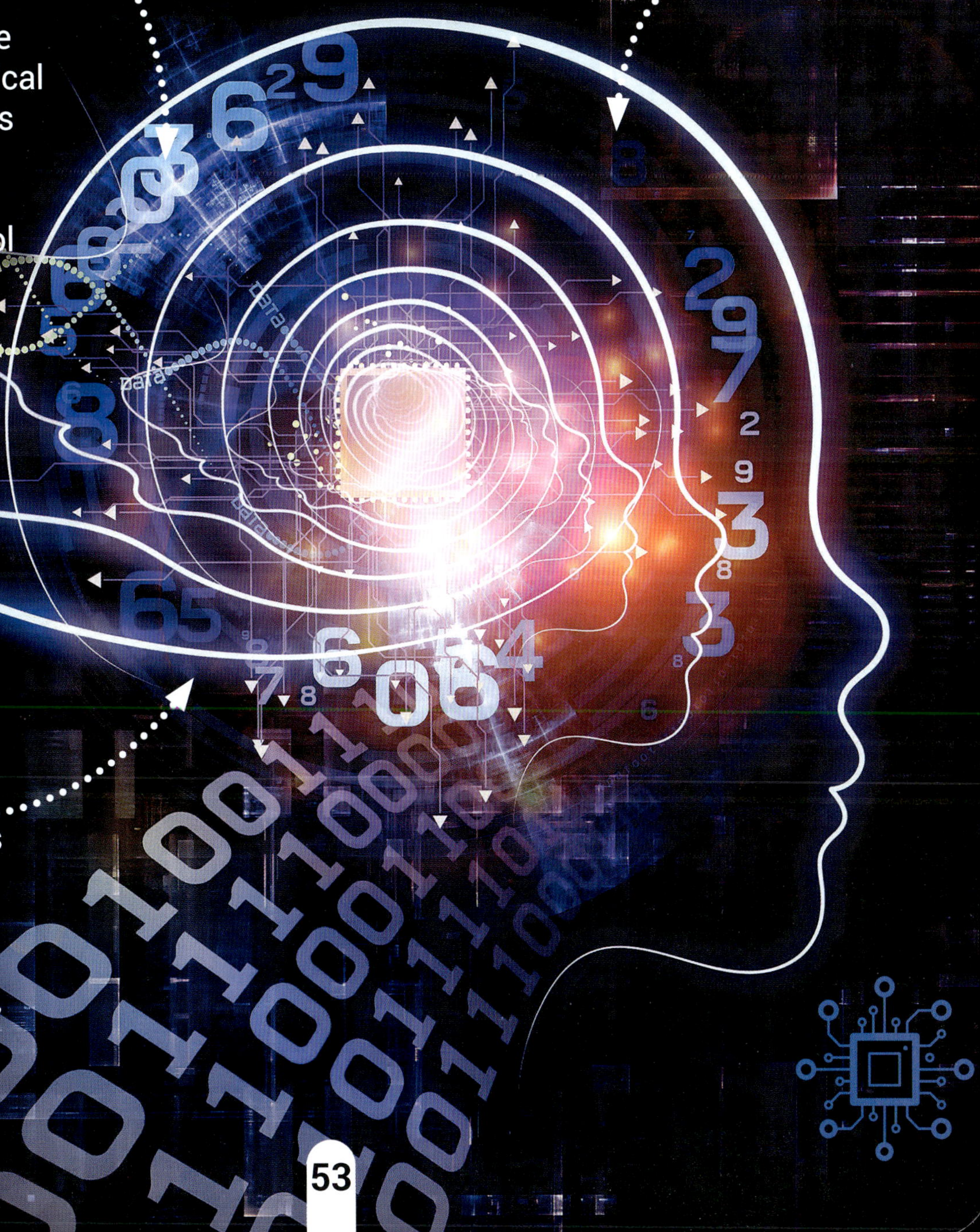

WHAT'S NEXT?

Future developments may include enhancing memory, operating devices remotely via thought, and even enabling brain-to-brain messaging.

What makes video games function?

Video games function through a mix of computer programs, graphics hardware, and player actions, creating exciting and responsive gameplay.

CORE DEVELOPMENT TOOLS

Game engines like Unity and Unreal Engine help developers create graphics, physics, and gameplay features.

POWERFUL VISUAL PROCESSING

Graphics Processing Units (GPUs) handle rendering, delivering smooth gameplay and realistic visuals.

PLAYER INTERACTION

Devices such as controllers and motion sensors let players control characters and explore virtual worlds in real time.

FUN FACT

GAMES LIKE MINECRAFT ARE NOW USED IN CLASSROOMS TO ENCOURAGE CREATIVITY AND TEAMWORK AMONG STUDENTS.

How is art created using technology?

Artists use digital tools like styluses and software to draw, paint, and animate on screens.

FUN FACT

DIGITAL ART PIECES, WHEN TURNED INTO NFTS, HAVE BEEN AUCTIONED FOR MILLIONS OF DOLLARS!

FORMS OF DIGITAL ART

You'll find 2D drawings, 3D models, animated scenes, and even art generated by computer algorithms.

BENEFITS AND PERKS

Digital art is easy to edit, share instantly online, and recreate without losing any of its original quality.

ARTIST'S TOOLKIT

Artists often work with graphic tablets, styluses, and powerful programs like Photoshop and Blender to bring their ideas to life.

What is telehealth or virtual healthcare?

Telehealth, also known as virtual healthcare, uses digital tools like video consultations and mobile apps to provide medical services from a distance. This method makes healthcare more accessible and convenient for patients.

HOW IT OPERATES

Patients connect with doctors using video calls, share health updates through apps, and get prescriptions digitally.

COMMON USES

Includes virtual doctor visits, fitness trackers monitoring heart rates, and therapy apps supporting mental health care.

BRAIN BUZZ

- What devices support virtual care?
- Can prescriptions be sent online?
- How does virtual medicine help doctors?

WHY IT'S HELPFUL

Saves travel time, offers healthcare access in remote locations, and ensures quick medical support.

How does digital technology support modern farming?

Digital technology helps modern farming by using tools like sensors, drones, and smart software to make agriculture more efficient and eco-friendly.

SMART FARMING IN ACTION

Sensors track soil moisture, drones check crop health, and AI studies weather to improve farming decisions.

REAL-WORLD APPLICATIONS

Farmers use mobile apps to plan planting, detect pests early, and make better choices for their crops.

WHY IT MATTERS

Digital farming saves water, cuts down waste, and boosts harvests for a more sustainable future.

FUN FACT

SOME DRONES ON FARMS SPRAY CROPS AND CHECK PLANT HEALTH FROM THE SKY!

How does a smart energy grid work?

A smart energy grid is a modern power system that uses digital technology to monitor, control, and optimize electricity delivery.

KEY ADVANTAGES

Minimizes blackouts, supports renewable energy sources, and lowers energy bills by promoting efficient power usage.

FUN FACT

DURING HEATWAVES OR STORMS, SMART GRIDS ADJUST ENERGY FLOW TO KEEP THE LIGHTS ON AND AVOID BLACKOUTS!

REAL-WORLD EXAMPLES

Households with solar panels can feed surplus electricity back into the grid, contributing to a cleaner, smarter energy network.

SYSTEM IN ACTION

Smart meters and sensors continuously monitor electricity use, while automated controls adjust energy flow to match demand instantly.

What are online payment systems?

Online payment systems allow people to send or receive money through electronic platforms without using cash.

BRAIN BUZZ

- What is a QR code payment?
- How safe are digital payments?
- Are digital payments eco-friendly?

PROCESS IN ACTION

Digital wallets such as PayPal and Google Pay securely hold funds, allowing users to make purchases online or at physical stores.

POPULAR METHODS

Examples include tap-and-go contactless payments, mobile banking apps, and cryptocurrency transactions.

WHY IT'S BENEFICIAL

Digital payments offer speed and ease of use and minimize the need to carry or handle cash.

A GUIDE TO TECHNOLOGY & INNOVATION TERMS

AI (ARTIFICIAL INTELLIGENCE)
Technology that makes machines think and learn like humans.

ALGORITHM
A set of instructions computers follow to solve problems or make decisions.

AR (AUGMENTED REALITY)
Technology that adds digital images or information to the real world, often through a smartphone or AR glasses.

ARTIFICIAL ORGANS
Man-made devices or tissues used to replace damaged body organs.

AUTONOMOUS ROBOTS
Machines that can perform tasks on their own without human help.

BCI (BRAIN-COMPUTER INTERFACE)
Technology that lets the brain control computers or machines directly.

BIOPRINTING
3D printing that creates living tissues or organs using special cells.

BLOCKCHAIN
A digital system for recording information securely across many computers.

BOT
A computer program that does automated tasks quickly and repeatedly.

BIOHACKING
Using technology and science to enhance the human body.

CARBON CAPTURE
Technology that traps and stores carbon dioxide from the air to reduce pollution.

CLOUD COMPUTING
Storing and accessing files, apps, and data over the internet instead of on your computer.

CRYPTOCURRENCY
Digital money like Bitcoin, which is secured by cryptography and works without a bank.

CYBERSECURITY
Methods used to protect computers, networks, and data from attacks or theft.

DIGITAL ASSISTANT
Voice-activated software like Siri or Alexa that helps with tasks.

DIGITAL FARMING
The use of technology like sensors and drones to improve farming methods.

DIGITAL PAYMENTS
Paying for things using apps, cards, or online systems without cash.

DIGITAL TWIN
A virtual copy of a real object or system used for testing and monitoring.

DRONE
A flying robot that can be controlled remotely or fly by itself.

EDGE COMPUTING
Processing data closer to where it's collected, speeding up decision-making.

EXOSKELETON
A wearable robotic suit that helps people move or lift things.

FILAMENT
The material used in 3D printers to build objects, like plastic or metal.

FIREWALL
A security system that protects computers from unauthorized access.

GENETIC ENGINEERING
Changing the genes of plants, animals, or humans to improve or alter them.

GPS (GLOBAL POSITIONING SYSTEM)
A satellite-based system that shows your exact location anywhere on Earth.

GREEN TECHNOLOGY
Tech that helps the environment by reducing pollution and saving energy.

HOLOGRAM
A 3D image that appears to float in space, created with light beams and lasers.

HYBRID CARS
Vehicles that use both gasoline and electric power to reduce pollution.

A GUIDE TO TECHNOLOGY & INNOVATION TERMS

IOT (INTERNET OF THINGS)
Everyday objects like fridges or watches connected to the internet, sharing data

MACHINE LEARNING
A type of AI that teaches machines to learn from data and improve over time.

MICROCHIP
A tiny computer chip that processes information.

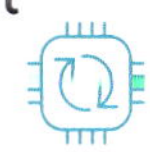

NANOBOT
A very tiny robot, smaller than a grain of sand, used in medicine and science.

NANOTECHNOLOGY
Science and technology done on a super small scale, like building things from atoms.

PROPELLER
A spinning blade that helps drones and ships move through the air or water.

QUANTUM COMPUTING
A new kind of super-powerful computing that uses quantum physics to process data faster.

QUANTUM INTERNET
A future internet system that uses quantum technology to make communication extremely secure.

RENEWABLE ARCHITECTURE
Designing buildings using eco-friendly materials and methods to save energy.

RENEWABLE ENERGY
Energy from sources that won't run out, like the sun, wind, and water.

RENEWABLE FUELS
Fuels made from plants or waste that can be replaced naturally

ROBOT
A machine that can be programmed to do tasks, sometimes without human help.

ROBOTICS IN MEDICINE
Using robots to help doctors with surgeries, treatments, and patient care.

SELF-DRIVING CAR
A car that drives itself using sensors, cameras, and AI.

SENSOR
A device that detects changes in the environment and sends the information to a machine.

SMART CITIES
Cities that use technology to manage resources like energy, traffic, and water efficiently.

SMART GRID
An advanced power network that automatically balances electricity supply and demand.

SMART HOME
A home with connected devices like lights, thermostats, and locks that you can control remotely.

SMART WEARABLES
Gadgets like fitness trackers or smartwatches that collect and share health or activity data.

TOUCHSCREEN
A display you can control with your fingers by tapping or swiping.

TELEMEDICINE (VIRTUAL MEDICINE)
Seeing doctors and getting health care through video calls and apps.

VIRTUAL REALITY (VR)
A computer-generated 3D world you can explore using special goggles or headsets.

VIDEO GAME
A digital game you can play on a computer, console, or phone.

VIRTUAL SHOPPING
Buying things online, sometimes with 3D or VR technology.

WI-FI
Wireless internet that lets devices connect to the web without cables.

WEARABLE TECHNOLOGY
Electronics you wear on your body, like smartwatches or fitness trackers.

SECRETS OF SMART TECHNOLOGY

THE FIRST COMPUTER WAS HUGE!

The ENIAC computer, built in 1945, was as big as a room and weighed over 27 tonnes!

SMARTPHONES ARE SUPERCOMPUTERS

A modern smartphone has more computing power than the computers used to land Apollo 11 on the Moon!

WI-FI USES RADIO WAVES

Wi-Fi sends information through the air using invisible radio waves, just like walkie-talkies!

5G IS ULTRA-FAST!

5G networks can be up to 100 times faster than 4G, making downloads almost instant.

THE CLOUD ISN'T IN THE SKY

Cloud storage means your data is saved on giant computers (servers) in special data centres.

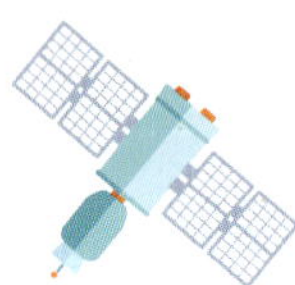

AI CAN RECOGNIZE FACES

Artificial intelligence helps your phone recognize your face to unlock it securely.

ROBOTS LEARN BY DOING

Some robots use machine learning to improve their tasks by practising over and over.

SELF-DRIVING CARS USE LASERS

Autonomous cars use laser scanners, called LiDAR, to "see" the road and avoid obstacles.

DRONES ARE PILOTED BY GPS

Drones can fly along set routes using GPS satellites, without a human controlling them.

EXOSKELETONS GIVE SUPER STRENGTH

Wearable exoskeletons help people lift heavy objects and assist in rehabilitation.

VR TRICKS YOUR BRAIN

Virtual Reality makes you feel like you're inside another world by showing each eye a slightly different image.

AR ADDS TO REAL LIFE

Augmented Reality layers fun extras on what you see, like digital dinosaurs in your backyard!

HOLOGRAMS LOOK 3D WITHOUT GLASSES

Holograms show 3D images that appear to float in space, no special glasses needed!

3D PRINTERS BUILD LAYER BY LAYER

3D printers create objects by adding one thin layer of material on top of another.

BIOPRINTERS PRINT HUMAN TISSUE

Scientists are using 3D printers to print real skin, bone, and even organs!

WEARABLE TECH TRACKS HEALTH

Smartwatches can count your steps, check your heart rate, and remind you to move!

SMART HOMES KNOW YOUR ROUTINE

Smart home gadgets can turn lights on when you walk in and make your house cozy before you arrive.

SMART CITIES HAVE SMART TRAFFIC

In smart cities, traffic lights can change based on real-time traffic to avoid jams.

DIGITAL TWINS ARE VIRTUAL COPIES

Digital twins are computer-made versions

SECRETS OF SMART TECHNOLOGY

of real things, like cars or buildings, used for testing and monitoring.

QUANTUM COMPUTERS ARE SUPERFAST

Quantum computers can solve problems in seconds that would take regular computers thousands of years.

BLOCKCHAIN KEEPS DATA SAFE

Blockchain technology stores data in blocks that are hard to change, making things like cryptocurrency secure.

CRYPTOCURRENCY IS DIGITAL MONEY

Bitcoin and other cryptocurrencies are forms of money that only exist online!

CYBERSECURITY PROTECTS YOUR INFO

Cybersecurity uses firewalls and encryption to keep hackers out of your personal data.

NANOBOTS ARE TINY HELPERS

Nanobots are so small they can travel through your bloodstream to deliver medicine!

SMART GRIDS SAVE ENERGY

Smart grids help deliver electricity more efficiently and use renewable energy sources.

DIGITAL PAYMENTS ARE FAST AND EASY

Mobile wallets and payment apps let you buy things instantly with just a tap or scan.

SPACE TOURISM HAS BEGUN!

Companies like SpaceX and Blue Origin are sending people into space for fun!

AI CAN CREATE ART

Artificial intelligence programs can paint pictures and even compose music!

VIRTUAL FARMING USES DRONES

Farmers use drones and sensors to monitor crops and water them precisely.

BRAIN-COMPUTER INTERFACES ARE REAL

Scientists are developing devices that let people control machines just by thinking!

ANSWERS

Here are the answers to the Brain Buzz questions in this book!

Page 4
- Internet and a camera.
- Yes. they track health.
- Electricity or batteries.

Page 6
- It's the brain.
- Rechargeable battery.
- Sensors detect touch.

Page 7
- Yes, but weaker.
- Router and internet.
- Yes, stronger signal.

Page 8
- Online space.
- Google Drive, Dropbox, iCloud.

Page 9
- Up to 100x faster.
- Yes, millions more.
- Cities, cars, factories.

Page 10
- Use Wi-Fi, send data, and share information.
- Needs security.
- Homes, hospital, farms, factories, and Smart cities.

Page 13
- Smart virtual helper.
- Through voice recognition.
- Yes, easily.

Page 15
- Non-player characters.
- Learns player moves.
- Yes, with coding.

Page 17
- Quantum encryption technology.
- Photons or qubits.
- Yes, instantly detectable.

Page 18
- A network of computers.
- Finances, healthcare, logistics.
- Yes, through transparency.

Page 21
- Smart homes, vehicles.
- Processes data locally.
- Yes, less data travel.

Page 22
- Electricity or batteries.
- Factories, hospitals, space.
- A flying robot.

Page 23
- Sensors and AI.
- Special test zones.
- Yes, with sensors.

Page 30
- Smartphones, tablets, AR glasses.
- Gamers, designers, doctors.
- Yes, interactive lessons.
- Yes, AR adds digital layers; VR creates virtual worlds.

Page 35
- Not completely secure.
- Possibly, but rare.
- Depends on usage.

Page 37
- Potentially, yes.
- A gene-editing tool.
- Generally, no.

Page 40
- A tiny particle.
- Still being studied.
- Smaller than cells.

Page 46
- Solar power.
- About 20-25 years.
- Mostly, yes.

Page 47
- Plants, algae, waste.
- Yes, eventually.
- Mostly, yes.

Page 50
- Carbon dioxide.
- Yes, as fuel.
- Yes, it reduces emissions.

Page 56
- Smartphones, tablets.
- Yes, digitally.
- Faster consultations.

Page 59
- Scan to pay.
- Highly secure.
- Yes, they are.